HFT Response to News an

Kara F. Rosier

Table of Contents

Abstract

I examine how high-frequency traders (HFTs) adjust their trading behavior based on market conditions, as well as their consequent market impact. I represent HFTs' trading behavior into two main categories of trading styles: *market-making*, whereby HFTs perform as "liquidity providers" in the Kyle (1985) model, and *active-trading*, whereby HFTs actively perform as "informed traders" in the Kyle framework. Analyzing HFTs' trading styles led to four novel findings. First, HFTs' market-making activities are negatively affected by both expected and unexpected stock volatility components. Second, during news events, HFTs select their trading styles across different news topics, based on the informativeness level of each topic. Third, due to the immediate active-trading strategies upon news events, HFTs facilitate price discovery only within around 100 seconds after news events. Lastly, the SEC's short-sale ban act in 2008 effectively restricted HFTs' active trading styles, but also excluded HFTs from improving the market price efficiency. Above all, understanding HFTs' market impact from their trading behavior, rather than mere trading speed, is essential to fully understanding their roles in the modern equities markets.

List of Tables

List of Figures

Chapter 1   Introduction

The emergence of high-frequency traders (hereafter, HFTs), that is, investors using computers to trade securities over extremely short time intervals, is a major change in the securities markets over the last decade. Nowadays, HFTs are one of the major players in the U.S. stock markets, accounting for more than 40% of NASDAQ dollar volume in 2009 (Hirschey (2014)). This situation has provoked heated debate about how to correctly define the role of HFTs in the equities markets, as well as about their overall contribution to the market quality.

According to the U.S. Securities and Exchange Commission (SEC), HFTs are characterized as "professional traders acting in proprietary capacity" who use "extraordinarily high-speed and sophisticated computer programs for generating, routing, and executing orders". Following this definition, the public has paid close attention on how HFTs engage in an arms race for a speed advantage in the scope of milliseconds in order to capture the most favorable quote in the stock market. However, in my paper, I argue that understanding HFTs' trading behavior, which is comparatively less discussed in previous academic studies, is crucial in correctly interpreting the source of HFTs' profit, and thus in gaining an understanding of their roles in affecting the market.

The current U.S. securities market is well-known for possessing a "maker-taker" structure. In this market, all trading participants can freely choose to perform as either liquidity-makers, who submit pending orders to the bid-ask order book (called "limit orders"), or liquidity-takers, who accept these pending orders (called "market orders") and then immediately complete trading transactions. Indeed, a higher trading speed can help HFTs to improve trading performance. By submitting orders faster than the other players, HFTs can either enjoy a higher priority in their limit order execution, or execute their market orders with the most favorable available prices. However, there is growing literature indicating that HFTs' trading activities are significantly affected by external market conditions, such as informed trading flows from institutional investors (van Kervel & Menkveld (2018)), order imbalances (Hirschey (2014)), quote improvements (Hasbrouck & Saar (2013)), or even macro events (Brogaard, Hendershott & Riordan (2014)). These findings, combined with the existence of a wide discrepancy in order execution preference (limit order VS market order) within different HFTs (Baron, Brogaard & Kirilenko (2012)), imply that a systematic understanding of HFTs' trading behavior is essential to recognizing their roles in and impact on the entire stock market.

Analysis of HFTs' trading behavior may also help to reconcile the heated debate about HFTs' market quality contribution. The majority of literature finds that HFTs mainly perform as liquidity-makers, who enhance market quality by submitting limit orders to both the bid and ask sides of the order book (Hagströmer & Nordén (2013), Brogaard, Hendershott & Riordan (2014)). Some researchers and practitioners, however, criticize HFTs as aggressive "liquidity-takers" who aggressively build short-term positions and thus lead to market instability, especially after witnessing a series of abnormal market events, including the "Flash Crash"[1] (see Kirilenko et al. (2017) and Brogaard et al. (2016)), "Knight-explosion"[2], and the "phantom liquidity" phenomenon, in which HFTs withdraw liquidity provision activities at the times when the market is in the direst need of liquidity (see Boehmer, Fong & Wu (2018)). My paper claims that the reasons behind these conflicting findings may originate in HFTs' superior trading skills, as HFTs attempt to exhibit different trading behaviors under different market conditions.

To provide a systematic view of how HFTs behave in different ways while seeking profits, I defined two main "trading styles" that characterize HFTs' trading activities. The first style is called *market-making*, fitting the role of market-makers in Kyle (1985), in which they provide liquidity to the market by accepting trading requests from other liquidity-takers. The other style is called *active-trading*, conforming to the role of informed-traders in the Kyle model, in which they trade on private information for returns. The analysis of HFTs' trading styles can be divided into two main questions.

The first main question is: *how are HFTs' different trading styles related to market conditions?* According to Kyle (1985), market-makers make trading price decisions by simultaneously balancing between gaining the liquidity premium by trading against noise-traders, and avoiding the loss of adverse selection by trading against informed traders. Furthermore, Drechsler, Moreira & Savov (2018) address the importance of stock volatility in affecting market-makers' willingness

---

[1] A flash crash is a very rapid, deep, and volatile fall in security prices that occurs within an extremely short period. HFTs are widely criticized as the cause of flash crash events, since HFTs can execute a large volume of trades within milliseconds, causing large market turbulence. Many flash crash events have occurred since HFTs have begun trading in U.S. stock markets, including the 2010 Dow Jones Flash Crash, the 2013 NASDAQ Flash Crashes, the 2014 U.S. Bond Flash Crash, the 2015 NYSE Flash Crash, etc.

[2] "Knight-explosion" refers to the 2012 stock trading disruption event, caused by a technical failure of the automated routing system from Knight Capital Group, one of the HFTs with the largest daily trading volume in the U.S. equity market. Knight's abnormal trading activities caused a significant disruption in the prices of 148 companies listed on the New York Stock Exchange, resulting in 4 million executions in 154 stocks, for more than 397 million shares, in approximately 45 minutes.

to trade: The private information held by informed traders becomes more valuable during periods of high market volatility, leading the trading flow to become more informative to future stock prices (therefore, producing a higher level of "Kyle's Lambda"). Thus, the concern for the issue of adverse-selection becomes more severe for market-makers during high volatility periods. Based on these frameworks, I validate HFTs' market-making roles from two perspectives. First, I measure HFTs' market-making style as the relationship between HFTs' net trading flow and the stock excess return, showing that the style coefficient is negative throughout the entire sample period, and the magnitude diminishes during periods of high market volatility. These results imply that HFTs' performs market-making roles by trading against the market flow, but their activities get dampened by a higher level of observable market volatility level. Second, HFTs' market-making return, proxied by the high-minus-low portfolio based on HFTs' trading flows across various stocks, is shown to be vulnerable to "volatility shock", as measured by the first-order difference of stock volatility in time-series. This result further validates the argument of Drechsler, Moreira & Savov (2018) by showing that, even if HFTs strategically alter their market-making intensity based on expected stock volatility level, their performance can still be hurt by the unexpected volatility component, which HFTs are unable to predict when making trading decisions.

HFTs' active-trading styles are identified from two perspectives, based on their consequential market impacts. The first is named *speculative-trading*, where HFTs' trading flow aligns with the direction of the next-minute stock price movement. This result aligns with the finding that HFTs' average holding period is less than two minutes (Kirilenko et al. (2017)), implying that HFTs' trading skills mainly focus on an extremely short time horizon. The second one is called *liquidity-timing*, referring to the relationship between HFTs' net flow and market liquidity measurements. Market liquidity is measured as the auto-correlation between the minute-wise stock return, with the null hypothesis of resting at zero levels under the perfect market liquidity condition, since all available market information should be immediately absorbed into price adjustments. My results showed that HFTs' trading flow actually worsens the liquidity measure, by finding that the auto-correlation of the stock return deviates more from zero, when HFTs' trading flow is strongly against the contemporaneous market flow. To align this pattern with HFTs' trading incentives, one possible explanation is that HFTs strategically time their liquidity-provision activities and charge for a higher liquidity premium, whenever they infer that the price fluctuation is driven by lack of liquidity rather than by private information.

The second main question is: *how do HFTs' different trading styles affect market quality?* By dissecting HFTs' trading activities into market-making and active-trading styles, I applied a news events study to test how HFTs exhibit different trading styles depending on different news information topics, and how these trading styles affect the consequent price discovery process. The results show a salient pattern that HFTs' trading styles are distinct dependent upon different types of news: HFTs only exhibit active-trading styles under "Informative News" topics (such as "Acquisition-mergers", "Analyst-ratings", etc.), while they only exhibit market-making styles under "Noisy news" topics (such as "Legal", "Technical-analysis", etc.). The mutually exclusive pattern of these trading styles reflects HFTs' incentives of trading on news information, accompanied by reducing market-making exposure, in order to avoid being picked off by other skillful traders (Copeland & Galai (1983)).

Next, to measure the effect of trading styles on market quality, I measured the contribution of HFT-initiated trades on the price discovery process after news events hit the market, by utilizing the identification strategy from Barclay & Warner (1993). I found that HFTs significantly facilitated prices discovery during news events: HFTs contributed to around 30% of the total price changes within 300s after events occur, which is significantly higher than the level of 10% during regular periods. The price discovery contribution is particularly strong when HFTs exert active-trading styles, as HFTs contribute to around 36% of total price changes within "Informative News" topics. Furthermore, by comparing the evolution of price discovery patterns, I found a sharp difference in how HFTs and non-HFTs behave differently in trading after news events. To be specific, HFT-initiated trades are shown to significantly facilitate the price discovery process only within the first 100 seconds after events, while non-HFT-initiated trades maintain their price discovery roles throughout the entire 300-second observation window. To align this finding with HFTs' trading incentives, I documented an inventory pattern that suggests that HFTs exert "back-running" strategies, similar to those in Yang & Zhu (2018), for profits: After news events, HFTs quickly increase their net inventory level, aligning with the direction of 300-second stock price movement, then gradually close the position throughout the time in order to lock in profits. In essence, HFTs' fast reaction towards news events brings them advantages in skimming profits from non-HFTs, and it also explains the reason that HFTs' active-trading strategies only transiently lead to price efficiency improvement after events.

To provide insights into how HFTs' trading styles provide policy-making implications, I analyze how market regulations, such as that SEC's short-sale ban act in 2008, affected the price discovery process after news events. The result shows that, during the regulation period, only HFTs' price discovery function is eliminated when stock prices drop after events. The result reflects the fact that HFTs' active-trading strategies become effectively constrained by regulation, since HFTs mainly rely on short-selling stocks to keep a temporary negative risk exposure, after negative news hits the market. Therefore, regulation may effectively stabilize the stock market by restricting HFTs' trading activities, but simultaneously deteriorate market efficiency by excluding HFTs from the price discovery process. Indeed, the dual effect of the SEC's short-sale restriction, in both reducing excessive market downside risk and worsening market quality, has been explored by several previous studies (Boehmer, Jones & Zhang (2013), Beber & Pagano (2013), and Grundy, Lim & Verwijmeren (2012)). However, none of these studies further identified the underlying reasons for these effects. My paper provides the answer by pointing out that HFTs are the key players affected by the SEC regulations, which consequently leads to these market impacts. Therefore, my study underscores the importance for policymakers to realize HFTs' trading behaviors when evaluating potential policy effects on the stock market.

My study emphasizes that an understanding of HFTs' trading behavior plays an important role in understanding HFTs' market impacts, which are not extensively investigated in previous literature. The traditional conception of HFTs are that their competition on relative trading speed, at the millisecond-level, brings them comparative advantages over other participants (Foucault, Kadan & Kandel (2013), Hendershott & Riordan (2012), Baron, Brogaard, Hagströmer & Kirilenko (2018)), but at the cost of market concentration and an inefficient and costly technological arms race (see Biais, Foucault & Moinas (2015) and Budish, Cramton & Shim (2015)). However, speed does not explain all, or even the majority, of HFTs' total revenue channel. In Baron, Brogaard, Hagströmer & Kirilenko (2018), the top 5 HFTs with the lowest trading latencies in NASDAQ OMX Stockholm exchange only accounted for 30% of the total profits of the entire HFT family, which implies that HFTs' trading skills may actually account for the major part of HFTs' total profits. In my paper, I validated the existence of HFTs' trading skills, by showing that all HFTs' trading styles are significant in the minute-scale level. Assuming HFTs merely use their speed advantage to trade ahead of other players in the scale of milliseconds, then the significance of all the styles metrics should vanish due to the time scale of my empirical design. In addition, I also show that HFTs' active-trading pattern actually lasts for nearly one minute after news events, which far exceeds the milli-second level where HFTs are perceived to mainly compete, and which is under the time scale that HFTs win over non-HFTs by exerting better trading decisions rather than faster trading speeds. All these findings prove the fact that the superior trading skills of HFTs, even without their speed advantages, can enable them to effectively skim profits from the market.

By analyzing the contingency of HFTs' trading styles on news information, my paper also sheds light on reconciling the controversial points of HFTs' contribution to market quality. My study utilizes a novel identification strategy, by using the heterogeneous information from news events as the external shock affecting the trading decisions for both HFTs and non-HFTs. This design is based on the findings that the "informative component" extracted from news information can effectively predict future stock price movements (see Tetlock (2007)), while the "noise component" from news, possibly due to the decrease of news quality over time or the inability of readers to correctly interpret complicated news, may also cause market turbulence (see Dugast & Foucault (2018)). My results show that the variation of weights between "information component" and "noise component" across news topics is the key factor in determining HFTs' choice of different trading styles, and that it leads to different impacts on HFTs' trading intensity, stock volatility, price efficiency, etc. Based on the fact that HFTs have no obligation in performing any specific roles in the stock market, the variation of HFTs' underlying trading styles may effectively explain the reason that previous studies, based on different market circumstances, led to conflicting views on HFTs' market quality contributions.

In addition, the unique feature of my dataset, combining both the real-time trading record and the news events information, enables me to accurately capture the trading behaviors of HFTs, rather than using other proxies as did previous studies. Therefore, my paper brings additional insights, or even conflicting opinions, on some findings discovered in previous literature, and it underscores the importance of utilizing correct identification strategies to study HFTs:

First, Drechsler, Moreira & Savov (2018) claimed that market-makers are negatively affected by both market volatility and volatility shocks. To replicate market-makers' trading activities, they used the daily-wise loser-minus-winner portfolio return as the proxy for market-makers' performance, claiming that this reversal strategy "mimics liquidity creation by buying stocks that go down and selling stocks that go up". However, one concern of their empirical design is that they do not observe the real-time positions from liquidity providers. Therefore, their proxy may fail to well represent the nature of market-makers' trading activities, where market-makers are highly sensitive to real-time market conditions rather than to inter-day stock information (see the results of this paper, and Brogaard, Hendershott & Riordan (2014)). In my study, by measuring HFTs' real-time market-making styles, I support the argument that HFTs, when exerting market-making styles, are indeed avoiding high-volatility period, and that HFTs' performances are harmed by unexpected volatility shocks.

Second, van Kervel & Menkveld (2018) found empirically that HFTs execute "predatory trading" strategies by learning private information from trading flows initiated by institutional investors. In essence, this implies that the information component in the trading flows can be extracted by HFTs for enhancing their trading performance. In my study, the introduction of HFTs' "liquidity-timing" style can be regarded as a robust version of van Kervel & Menkveld's findings, in that HFTs' trading flow can bring extra prediction power on future stock return after interacting with the trading flow from the entire market, rather than just from specific players. In addition, the significance of the trading styles is robust across my entire sample period, rather than only within the hours where institutional investor "executes a series of child trades".

Third, Hasbrouck & Saar (2013) utilized NASDAQ ITCH dataset, containing all real-time order records, but without the label of traders' identities, to claim that HFTs' trading activities reduce stock volatility. However, without labels explicitly identifying HFTs, Hasbrouck and Saar define a "strategic run" pattern in the order feed data, containing consecutive series of alternating submission, cancellation, and execution records in short time period, as the order records from HFTs' trading algorithm. However, the "strategic run" pattern should be better interpreted as a proxy only for measuring HFTs' market-making activities, since HFTs would quickly submit and cancel limit orders to detect the trading incentives from the order flow. In fact, my event study shows that HFTs' market-making styles indeed reduces stock volatility; their active-trading styles, however, are accompanied with an increasing level of stock volatility. Therefore, my result again emphasizes the importance of correctly identifying HFTs' trading activities before making conclusions about their market impact.

The chapters are as follows. Chapter 2 introduces the datasets used for study and summary statistics. Chapter 3 analyzes HFTs' market-making and active-trading styles, based on market conditions. Chapter 4 shows HFTs' heterogeneous trading styles across different news topics. Chapter 5 discusses HFTs' contribution to the price discovery process upon news events. Chapter 6 concludes. All tables and figures are listed in the appendix.

Chapter 2   Dataset and Summary Statistics

2.1 NASDAQ HFT Dataset

To measure real-time trading styles for both HFTs and non-HFTs, in this study I use NASDAQ HFT Dataset for academics under a non-disclosure agreement. This dataset covers all trading records executed in NASDAQ, among 120 selected stocks listed in NYSE and NASDAQ and all trading days from the Year 2008 to 2009. All trade records in the dataset are executed against either displayed or hidden liquidity during market hours or non-market hours in NASDAQ exchange, but not executed in other market venues.

The sample categorizes stocks into three market capitalization groups: large, medium, and small. Each size group contains 40 stocks. The large-size category is composed of 40 of the largest market capitalization stocks (e.g., Apple, GE). The medium-size category consists 40 stocks around the 1000th largest one in the Russell 3000 (e.g., Foot Locker), and the small-size category contains 40 stocks around the 2000th largest one in the Russell 3000.

For each trade record in the dataset, the key variables include:

1. Stock symbol;

2. Date;

3. Timestamp (in milliseconds);

4. Traded shares;

5. Execution price;

6. Buy-sell indicator, with "B" or "S" indicating trading activities based on the liquidity-taker. "B" means the liquidity-taker trades the stock as a buyer, and "S" means the liquidity-taker trades the stock as a seller.

7. Identities of the liquidity-taker and liquidity-maker for each trade: All trades are classified into four types: HH, HN, NH, NN. For each type of trades, the first letter indicates the identity of liquidity-taker, and the second letter states the identity of liquidity-maker. "N" indicates that the identity of the trading participant is a non-HFT and "H" indicates that

the identity is an HFT (for instance, "HN" means the liquidity-taker is an HFT, and the liquidity-maker is a non-HFT).

In this dataset, the HFT firms are identified by NASDAQ under their knowledge of their customers and analysis of firms' trading pattern, such as how often a firm's net trading in a day crosses zero, its order duration, and its order-to-trade ratio. However, several caveats need to point out before analyzing this dataset:

First, the NASDAQ HFT Dataset cannot cover all HFT firms. According to Brogaard, Hendershott & Riordan (2014), this dataset only contains 26 HFTs who should be regarded as proprietary trading firms. Therefore, some other trading firms that act as brokers for customers or engage in proprietary lower-frequency trading strategies (such as Goldman Sachs and Morgan Stanley) are not identified as HFTs, and HFTs who route their orders through these firms are excluded as well.

Second, this dataset only classifies trading participants into two main categories (HFTs and non-HFTs), without identifying each individual HFT firm (or non-HFT firm as well). By regarding all HFTs as a whole to represent HFTs' aggregate trading behavior, this may omit the potential differences of trading styles within HFT firms. For example, Baron, Brogaard & Kirilenko (2012) studies 31 HFT firms and show that 10 of them complete more than two thirds of their trades with market orders, while 10 other firms complete almost 90% of their trades with limit orders. Biais & Foucault (2014) also classifies HFT trading strategies in different groups and discusses their heterogeneous consequence of market impact. Therefore, the limit of data excludes me from realizing the heterogeneity of trading behavior and speed across different HFT firms, and make it impossible for me to analyze HFTs' trading styles upon controlling each individual HFT firm.

Third, this dataset only includes all trading transactions in NASDAQ, which may miss detecting some cross-market trading activities for some HFTs. For example, Menkveld (2013) shows that by analyzing HFTs' trading activities in Euronext and Chi-X, HFTs' aggregate inventory position from these two markets shows a mean-reverting pattern, while the position in each market does not. This result underscores the importance of considering HFTs' trading patterns from various trading venues, which unfortunately cannot be captured by the NASDAQ HFT Dataset. To validate the homogeneity of trading styles across U.S. trading venues, it is important to emphasize the fact that unlike European markets, all trading players in U.S. exchanges, no matter HFTs or non-

HFTs, cannot voluntarily choose the exchanges they want to execute their order in. Since 2005, the Securities and Exchange Commission (SEC) passed the Regulation National Market System (Reg NMS), and stipulated in "Rule 611" that all trades are required to be re-routed by the exchanges to the one with the most favorable bid and ask prices among all exchanges (called "protected quotes"). Therefore, all other exchanges with less favorable bid-ask prices will be "locked" until the more favorable quotes are cleared from the market. This rule effectively enables the trading processes to become integrated within the entire U.S. market, since all traders, including HFTs, must trade stocks irrespective of the listing locale. To further validate this point, O'Hara & Ye (2011) also shows that competition between market centers has effectively removed the bias of trading styles in the current fragmented market structure. Additionally, the prevalence of Inter-market Sweep Orders executed by HFTs (see Chakravarty et al. (2012)) also confirms that HFTs' technology arm-race focuses on getting the most favorable execution price quotes across all venues, rather than which specific exchange they prefer to trade in. Therefore, all evidence mentioned above validates that the trading patterns from our NASDAQ HFT Dataset can be perceived to represent the general pattern across all trading venues in the U.S. market.

[Insert Table 1 here.]

Table 1 shows the summary statistics of the dataset, with all numbers listed with the average level per stock per trading day. All trade records are further sub-grouped into columns by the trade types (All, HH, HN, NH, NN) and rows by the size of stocks measured by market capitalization (All, Large, Middle, Small). Within each subgroup, "Trades" represents the number of trading records, "Shares" represents trading shares (in thousands), and "Dollar" represents dollar volume traded (in millions). Based on the table, we can observe the following findings:

First, by comparing trading statistics across different sizes of stocks, we can see that most trades occur within large stocks: Under "All" Column, large stocks account for 85.3% of all trading records, 92.9% of all trading shares, and 89.5% of all dollar volume.

Second, HFTs are involved with a significant fraction of all trades executed in NASDAQ. By looking at "All Stocks" Row, we can find that among all trades, nearly 40% of all trades are with HFTs as liquidity-takers (by summing up trades from HH and HN) or liquidity-makers (by summing up trades from HH and NH), which is similar to the level from Brogaard, Hendershott & Riordan (2014). Therefore, the substantial fraction of labeled HFT trades in our dataset indicates the analytical results in later chapters should well represent all existing HFTs in the stock market.

Third, HFTs focus more on trading among large stocks. Figure 1 further shows the fraction of shares (or trades) where the liquidity-takers are HFTs. The result indicates that among large stocks, HFTs participate in around 45% of all trades as liquidity-takers, which is significantly higher than the results in middle and small stocks. Though not shown in this paper, the fraction of trades where HFTs are liquidity-makers also shows a similar pattern among different sizes of stock subgroups. All these results are intuitive: since HFTs mainly seek profits from second-level stock price fluctuations, HFTs should prefer more on stocks with the larger absolute level of transient stock price movements and market depth, which are typically larger stocks with higher daily volume and price level. Previous literature also made similar arguments based on other independent datasets, such as Hirschey (2014), Kirilenko et al. (2017) and Menkveld (2013). These conclusions are important in that it will help to explain the regression results in the next chapter, where I compare HFT's trading styles among different stock size subgroups.

[Insert Figure 1 here.]

2.2 RavenPack News Analytics

RavenPack News Analytics (hereafter, "RavenPack") is a database providing news data and comprehensive list of analysis results on each piece of news information. The uniqueness of this database is that it includes the news publish time with timestamp accuracy in milliseconds, compared with other traditional datasets (such as Factiva, Thompson Reuters or Bloomberg) only with timestamp accuracy in minutes. The high level of timestamp accuracy is important in HFT studies, since both HFTs and non-HFTs may react fast as within seconds after news gets published.

For the research purpose of this paper, I selected 25,419 news events under the following selection criteria, based on the variables provided for each news in the dataset:

- The *NAME_ENTITY* variable labels firm names that are in one of the 120 stocks in HFT

Dataset (to ensure the content of each news indeed relates to stocks covered in NASDAQ HFT Dataset);

- The *Date* variable is between 01/01/2008 to 12/31/2009 (to match with the time range covered by NASDAQ HFT Dataset);

- The *Timestamp* variable (in EST Time) is between 9:30 a.m. to 4:00 p.m. (to only select news events happen during the market hour of NASDAQ);

- The *RELEVANCE* variable is with the value greater or equal to 75 (to ensure news events being highly relevant with target stocks);

- The *G_ENS* variable, measuring the novelty of news, should reach the highest level as 100 (to ensure no stale news exists. So for each news event selected, its contents will be unexpected to all trading players, assuming there is no insider information before news get published).

Based on these selection criteria, in Table 2 I list the frequency statistics for all news events selected from RavenPack. All news are categorized in terms of *Group* variable and sentimental direction (*CSS*) provided by RavenPack. RavenPack automatically categorizes all news into 2,000 topic categories following a multi-layer structure, with labels on each layer representing news topics under different refinery levels (For example, one piece of news may have "business" in variable *Topic*, "technical-analysis" in variable *Group*, "technical-view" in variable *Type*, and "technical-view-bullish" in variable *Category*). The sentimental direction of news is directly from "Composite Sentiment Score" (*CSS*) provided from RavenPack. According to RavenPack Userguide, news events are defined as positive if $CSS > 50$, negative if $CSS < 50$, and neutral if $CSS = 50$. Among all news selected from RavenPack, in Table 2 I show that 8,084 news in "Positive news" group, 5,485 news in "Negative news" group, and 11,850 news in "Neutral News" group.

[Insert Table 2 here.]

One important thing to point out is: According to RavenPack User Guide, For each news event, all variables listed above are given based on the inference from historical news events and their consequent market impact *before* this event happens. Therefore, the rules for constructing variables effectively excluded the potential forward-looking bias, when I study HFTs' trading patterns upon news events in later chapters.

Chapter 3   Classification of HFT Trading Styles: Do HFTs operate as Kyle liquidity providers or do they help inject information into prices?

In this chapter, I am going to define metrics for measuring the trading styles of HFTs for three main purposes. First, since previous literature shows the large variety of trading styles that different HFTs specialized in (Baron, Brogaard & Kirilenko (2012)), I am trying to check whether these trading styles can also be identified under the most general circumstances, i.e., based on the entire sample period rather than on specific events. Second, studying HFTs' trading styles may also produce new findings that supplement the current literature, such as how HFTs' market-making styles are affected by stock volatility (Drechsler, Moreira & Savov (2018)). Third, these measures of trading styles will be applied to events study in later chapters, in order to examine changes in HFTs' trading styles amidst news events, as well as their subsequent impact on price discovery.

One important feature of the NASDAQ HFT Dataset is that it explicitly shows whether the trading participant is an HFT or non-HFT, for both the liquidity-taking and liquidity-making sides of each trade. Therefore, it attempts to first look at the overall return performance across all trades, differing by the identities of trading participants. Due to the lack of firm-level identities of trading participants from the dataset, one constraint of this test is the lack of holding period for calculating the realized return levels. Therefore, in Figure 2, I instead show the return trajectories of different types of trades, under the assumption of various liquidation horizons. I categorize all trades into four distinct subgroups: HH, HN, NH, NN, with the first (second) letter showing the identity of liquidity-taker (liquidity-maker). For example, HN means the liquidity-taker of a trade is an HFT, and the corresponding liquidity-maker is a non-HFT. The X-axis represents the log-value of the liquidation time horizon after trades happen (from 0s to 500s), and the Y-axis represents the volume-weighted, fee-adjusted average percentage return for the liquidity-taker of trades. I calculate the return in round-trade fashion, that is, for a buy(sell)-trade, its return is calculated as if the trading position were reverted at the liquidation time, based on the real-time National Best Bid and Offer (NBBO) price level. The Dashed lines represents 95% confidence intervals of return level estimation. In the plot, we can observe four primary patterns:

First, all trades initially generate negative round-trade return, which is equivalent to paying the bid-ask spread. Moreover, all trade returns show an increasing pattern when the liquidation horizon is extended. This pattern implies that liquidity-takers, on average, have skills to predict short-term stock return, regardless of whether they are either HFTs or non-HFTs.

Second, the trend of increasing return level only persists to around 100 seconds after trade executions, implying that the optimal holding period for traders to utilize the short-term trading skills is between one to two minutes. To support this finding, Kirilenko et al. (2017) proved that HFTs' inventory exhibits a unique reversal pattern in minute-level time horizon, by showing that HFTs' next-minute trading flow is significantly negative with the past-minute inventory level, and HFTs reduce half of their holdings in less than two minutes on average.

Third, when the identities of both liquidity-takers and liquidity-makers are HFTs (or non-HFTs), the average return from liquidity-takers is closed to zero levels at maximum, when holding periods last between one and two minutes. The pattern is also intuitive, as an equality of trading skills on both sides of trades, should ensure an equilibrium in the trading return between liquidity-takers and liquidity-makers.

Fourth, HN (NH) trades have significantly higher (lower) round-trade return across all four subgroups. This pattern implies that HFTs, typically perceived to have better trading skills, hold advantages when trading against non-HFTs. We can see that HN trades generate net return by one basis point at the maximum level, which is similar in magnitude to the findings of Hendershott (2011). On the other hand, although it is possible that non-HFTs can generate positive raw return when taking liquidity from HFTs, the net return after adjusting the rebate fees never rises above zero across all liquidation horizons, and it only reaches around -0.7 basis point at maximum. These results also validate the incentives for HFTs to supply liquidity to the market – even at the risk of being adversely selected by non-HFTs – as long as the market rebates fee[3] they receive from providing liquidity can fully cover the expected loss from trading against non-HFTs. To summarize, all these results imply that HFTs have trading skills superior to those of non-HFTs, on both the liquidity-taking and liquidity-making sides of trades.

---

[3] "Market rebates" are fees set by exchanges, in order to attract order flow by incentivizing liquidity-makers to provide liquidity at the most competitive prices. NASDAQ adopts a fee structure where a per-share rebate level is set for all trades executed in NASDAQ. If an execution occurs, the liquidity-maker receives a rebate by $0.0025 per share, and the liquidity-taker executing against that limit order pays a fee to the market by $0.003 per share.

[Insert Table 2 here.]

3.1 Analysis of HFTs' trading style: Market-making

HFTs are widely assumed to perform a market-making role in modern equity markets. Extant research has shown that the presence of HFTs is associated with improvements in market quality, including lower bid-ask spreads and improved price efficiency (See Menkveld (2013), Hagströmer & Nordén (2013); Brogaard, Hendershott & Riordan (2014); and Jovanovic & Menkveld (2016)). However, some research also shows that HFTs strategically withdraw liquidity provision to avoid bearing excessive losses from being adversely selected by liquidity-takers (See Boehmer, Fong & Wu (2018)). Therefore, it is essential to design empirical methods to quantify the extent of HFTs' market-making trading style, and to analyze the relationship between HFTs' market-making activities and various market conditions.

To ensure that the empirical design validates HFTs' market-making role, my main objective is to see whether HFTs' general trading style is consistent with the liquidity providers' function defined in Kyle (1985) and other relevant studies. To be specific, the arguments I need to validate empirically are listed as follows:

1. **HFTs provide liquidity in the opposite direction of temporary price movement.** In the Kyle model, assuming that no players have any private information about future stock value in the market, market-makers always trade against order flow by providing liquidity to liquidity-takers. Market-makers profit from the reversal of stock price afterward, due to the temporary price deviation from underlying value caused by liquidity-taking trades from noise traders.

2. **HFTs reduce liquidity provision during times of high stock volatility.** According to Drechsler, Moreira & Savov (2018), insiders with private information have more information gain when stock volatility is higher. Therefore, by extending the Kyle model, they argue that market-makers are discouraged from providing liquidity during high-volatility periods, due to higher expected losses from being adversely selected by informed traders.

3. **As market-makers, HFTs generate less realized return if volatility shock is more significant.** Following the previous argument, when market-makers set their optimal liquidity provision level based on current market conditions, a more substantial level of "volatility shock",

measured by the unexpected part of future volatility based on historical stock volatility condition, can cause market-makers to lose from being adversely selected to a greater extent by trading counterparties.

In order to validate the first two points, I designed the identification strategy as follows. For observations measured at the beginning of every minute during the market hours of NASDAQ, within each trading day and for each available stocks covered by the dataset, I employed the following panel regression:

$$HFT\_Flow_{t,t+60}^i = \alpha + \beta_0 \tilde{R}_{t-60,t}^i + \beta_1 RV_{t-300,t}^i + \beta_2 RV_{t-300,t}^{MKT}$$

$$+ \gamma(RV_{t-300,t}^i * \tilde{R}_{t-60,t}^i) + \eta(RV_{t-300,t}^{MKT} * \tilde{R}_{t-60,t}^i) + \kappa_i X_i + \varepsilon, \qquad (1)$$

where the net flow of HFTs, denoted as HFT_Flow, is defined as follows:

$$HFT\_Flow_{t_1,t_2}^i = \sum_{trade \in (t_1,t_2)} HN_B^i - HN_S^i - NH_B^i + NH_S^i \qquad (2)$$

and the return variation, RV, is defined as follows:

$$RV_{t-300,t}^i = stdev\{R_s^i \text{ for } s \text{ in } \{t-300, t-290, ..., t-10, t\}\} \qquad (3)$$

In Eq. 1, $HFT\_Flow_{t_1,t_2}$ represents the net flow HFTs trade on stock i from time t_1 to t_2 (in seconds); $\tilde{R}_{t_1,t_2}^i$ is the excess return of stock i; and X_i represents stock fixed effect. Due to the large difference of average trading volume across different stocks, I normalized all HFTs' net flow with the average minute volume from the past five trading days. To measure the stock and market volatility in short time horizons, I defined RV as a proxy by measuring the standard deviation of stock return (or market portfolio) for every 10 seconds from $t-300s$ to ts. Furthermore, to obtain the available high-frequency-level price data from the market portfolio, I used the S&P 500 ETF Trust (NYSE: SPY) from the TAQ Dataset as the proxy for market return. Finally, I calculated all return levels with midpoint-to-midpoint metrics.

In the regression above, the β_0 coefficients, measuring the sensitivity of HFTs' trading flow against the stock return level, reflect HFTs' market-making styles. Following the Kyle model, a larger magnitude of β_0 coefficients indicate that: When the information component from the trading flow (i.e., "Kyle's Lambda") is smaller, HFTs would make a smaller amount of price adjustment in order to accept a given volume of order request from liquidity takers. Therefore, in equilibrium, a larger magnitude of β_0 coefficients essentially represents HFTs exert market-making style to a greater extent.

Table 3 shows the regression results. Columns (1) to (4) list results when regression was applied to all 120 stocks in the dataset, or the 40 large/middle/small stocks only. All observations were measured at the beginning of each minute during market hours, per stock per trading day. Due to the large number of total observations, for each regression, I randomly selected four million observations from the entire sample via bootstrapping. Column (1) clearly shows that the past-minute stock excess return has a significant negative prediction power on HFTs' net flow in the next minute: one standard deviation of the increase of stock excess return reduces HFTs' net flow by 339.3 shares. In addition, by looking at the interaction term between past return variation and past excess return, we can see that a higher level of return variation, either in terms of stock return or market return, dampens the reversal pattern of HFTs' net flow. Comparing column (2), (3) and (4), we can further see that market-making coefficients are more significant with large stocks, which matches with the evidence in Figure 1 that HFTs take a larger fraction of trading shares among large stocks.

To further quantify the dependency of HFTs' market-marking styles on stock volatility, I modified Eq. 1 as follows:

$$
\begin{aligned}
HFT\_Flow_{t,t+60}^i &= \alpha + \beta_0 \tilde{R}_{t-60,t}^i + \beta_1 RV_{t-300,t}^i + \beta_2 RV_{t-300,t}^{MKT} \\
&+ \gamma_1 \tilde{R}_{t-60,t}^i * 1\{\text{Middle} RV_{t-300,t}^i\} + \gamma_2 \tilde{R}_{t-60,t}^i * 1\{\text{High } RV_{t-300,t}^i\} \\
&+ \eta_1 \tilde{R}_{t-60,t}^i * 1\{\text{Middle } RV_{t-300,t}^{MKT}\} + \eta_2 \tilde{R}_{t-60,t}^i * 1\{\text{High } RV_{t-300,t}^{MKT}\} + \kappa_i X_i + \varepsilon,
\end{aligned}
$$

$$(4)$$

where "Middle" represents dummies where the return variation of stock i (or market portfolio) is within the top 20~50% among all observations of the same stock (or market portfolio) throughout the entire sample period, and "High" represents dummies where the return variation is among the top 20%. Therefore, the interaction terms capture the extra effect on the reversal pattern of HFTs' future net flow, during middle- or high-volatility periods. Results are shown in columns (5) to (8) in Table 3. Again, we can see that the increase of return variation significantly reduces HFTs' reversal pattern on future net flow, with the effect being most significant among large stocks. In column (5), for example, one standard deviation of increase in stock past excess return decreases the future 60s HFT net flow by 136.91/112.08/77.77 shares when stock return variation is low/middle/high, and one standard deviation of increase in stock past excess return decreases future 60s HFT net flow by 84.95/61.91/3.54 shares when market return variation is low/middle/high. Thus, the results in Table 3 validate both Point 1 and Point 2 about the patterns of HFTs' performance as market-makers in the stock market.

[Insert Table 3 here.]

One concern is that the empirical design in Eq. 1, by predicting HFTs' next-minute trading flow based on past-minute market conditions, does not align with the market-makers' role in Kyle (1985). in the Kyle model, market-makers decide the trading price at the same time when liquidity-takers submit their requests for trading shares, rather than with the minute-level time lag. In reality, however, HFTs should have some latency in evaluating the market conditions before deciding their market-making strategies, rather than functioning as perfect liquidity providers in the Kyle model. Nevertheless, to alleviate this concern, in Table 4 I modified the regression formula in Eq. 1 by replacing $HFT\_Flow^i_{t,t+60}$ with $HFT\_Flow^i_{t-60,t}$, in order to measure the relationship between HFTs' trading flow and the contemporaneous market conditions. All previous results from Table 3 persists in Table 4 and with even more significant coefficients, implying that my original empirical design, though with time lags, did not affect the measured HFTs' market-making characteristics.

[Insert Table 4 here.]

In order to validate the third point, which contends that HFTs lose when the volatility shock is larger, I tested the relationship between the long-short portfolio, based on HFTs' trading flow, and the magnitude of volatility shock. Empirically, I first constructed the HFT high-minus-low (HML) portfolio by ranking stocks based on their past-minute normalized HFT flow, then longed the top-tercile stocks and shorted bottom-tercile stocks, weighted by market capitalization of each stock. The portfolio was held for 60 seconds, with return denoted as $R_{t,t+60}^{H-L}$. Following this method, the long-short portfolio strategy was re-weighted for every 60 seconds, based on the normalized HFT flow during the last minute. After measuring the performance of the long-short portfolio in time series fashion, I performed the regression that follows:

$$R_{t,t+60}^{H-L} = \alpha + \beta R_{t,t+60}^{MKT} + \gamma(RV_{t,t+60}^{MKT} - RV_{t-300,t}^{MKT}) + \varepsilon_m, \tag{5}$$

where $RV_{t,t+60}^{MKT} - RV_{t-300,t}^{MKT}$ captures the magnitude of volatility shock, by computing the increase of return variation from the past 300 seconds to the future 60 seconds.

Table 5 shows the regression results. Columns (1) and (2) were generated by calculating HFTs' HML portfolio based on all 120 stocks in the sample, while columns (3) to (5) apply HML strategies based on 40 large/middle/small stocks only. Across all columns, we can see that the return of HML portfolio is negatively affected by contemporaneous market excess return. For example, in column (2), the increase of market excess return by one standard deviation leads to a decrease of HML portfolio return by 1.63 basis points (or 0.23 standard deviation). At the same time, we can also find that the level of volatility shock negatively affects the HML portfolio return. Though the magnitude of coefficients is only 0.254, after taking the standard deviation of volatility shock into account, the increase of volatility shock level by one standard deviation leads to a decrease of HML portfolio return by 1.41 basis points (or 0.20 standard deviation). Furthermore, the impact of volatility shock on HFTs' profitability is again most significant on large stocks. In column (3), when HML portfolio is constructed only among 40 large stocks, the increase of volatility shock level by one standard deviation leads to a decrease of HML portfolio return by 1.83 basis points (or 0.24 standard deviation). Due to the finding that the magnitude of impact on HFTs' return from volatility shock is comparable to that from market excess return, volatility shock should be regarded as an important factor affecting HFTs' market-making behavior.

[Insert Table 5 here.]

To address some main concerns, I carried out two sets of robust tests: First, the current return metric for measuring the return from HML strategy may not well represent HFTs' profitability. This is because the current metric only measures the portfolio return from each stock component starting *after* the portfolio is constructed, a construct that ignores the short-term price change within the period after HFTs' trades but *before* the time point of constructing the HML portfolio. Therefore, due to the nature of the short holding period for HFTs, the existing results may significantly change after taking this missing component of return into account. To solve this issue, when calculating HFT high-minus-low return $R_{t,t+60}^{H-L} = (P_{t+60} - P_t)/P_t$ for each stock in the portfolio, I replaced P_t with $\tilde{P}_t$:

$$\tilde{P}_t = \frac{\sum_{HFTtrade \in (t-60,t)} S_i * P_i}{\sum_{HFTtrade \in (t-60,t)} S_i}, \tag{6}$$

The initial price is now calculated as the average execution price during the past 60 seconds, rather than the stock mid-price at the moment of portfolio construction. Table 6 lists the robust testing results, with all other steps identical to those in Table 5. From Table 6, we can see that all previous conclusions still hold, since regression results are highly similar to the ones shown in Table 5.

[Insert Table 6 here.]

Second, the R^2 among all regressions in Table 5 are very low as below 0.01, while the economic magnitudes of the explanatory variable coefficients are very large. Though more detailed analysis will be covered in the next subsection regarding how the time horizon of prediction affects the magnitude of R^2, basically, a longer horizon for prediction analysis can smooth more data noises and thus reveal a stronger R^2, which explains why using minute-level high-minus-low portfolio regression lead to a relatively small magnitude of R^2 even if the causal relationship holds. To validate this logic, in Table 7 I performed a similar analysis with day-level observations, to further show my result is robust in terms of time horizon and different proxies measuring volatility shocks. To be specific, the following regression is designed as follows:

$$R_m^{H-L} = \alpha + \beta R_m^{MKT} + \gamma \Delta VIX_m + \varepsilon_m, \tag{7}$$

where ΔVIX is defined as:

$$\Delta VIX_m = VIX_m - VIX_{m-1}, \tag{8}$$

In Eq. 7, the HFT high-minus-low portfolio is constructed similarly, but now the return R_m^{H-L} is calculated as the cumulative daily return of this minute-wise high-minus-low strategy. ΔVIX captures the volatility shock, by measuring the increase of VIX Index from the previous day to the current day, with data collected from the CBOE Indexes Database in WRDS. In Table 7, we can again see that both the market excess return and the surprise volatility term show significantly negative coefficient among all stocks, with the effect particularly strong among large stocks. In column (2), an increase of market excess return by one standard deviation decreases HML daily return by 0.22% (or 0.17 standard deviation), while an increase of VIX Index by one standard deviation decreases HML daily return by 0.26% (or 0.21 standard deviation). In addition, note that the R^2 is now around 0.01, which is nearly 10 times larger than the level shown in Table 5.

[Insert Table 7 here.]

To summarize, I conclude that HFTs' trading pattern aligns with the role of market-makers based on previous literature. In general, HFTs supply liquidity to the market by trading in the opposite direction of the market flow. However, HFTs' market-making activities are diminished when market volatility is high, and HFTs suffer losses from volatility shocks, due to more severe adverse selection by informed traders.

3.2 Analysis of HFTs' trading style: Active-trading

Discussion about HFTs' active-trading strategies is relatively limited in previous literature, in which HFTs generate trading signals mainly based on the trading flows from large institutional investors (See Brunnermeier & Pedersen (2005), Yang & Zhu (2018), van Kervel & Menkveld (2018)), macro events (see Brogaard, Hendershott and Riordan (2014)), imbalances of orders between the bid and ask side of the order book, or even temporary pricing discrepancies across similar assets (see Chaboud et al. (2014)).

In this chapter, I designed two different ways to quantify the level of HFTs' active-trading styles, based on their market impact from different perspectives. The first method, called *speculative-trading*, directly tests HFTs' profitability level by measuring the prediction power of their trading flow on future stock return level. The regression formula was designed as follows:

$$\tilde{R}^i_{t,t+60} = \alpha + \beta \tilde{R}^i_{t-60,t} + \phi HFT\_Flow^i_{t-60,t} + \kappa_i X_i + \varepsilon, \tag{9}$$

where $\tilde{R}$ represents stock excess return; HFT_Flow represents HFTs' net trading flow as defined in Eq. 2, after being normalized by the average minute-wise trading volume during the past five trading days; and X_i captures stock fixed effect. Therefore, the coefficient ϕ represents informed traders' role in the Kyle model, by effectively capturing HFTs' ability of predicting future return based on their short-term trading skills.

The second method, called *liquidity-timing*, provides an indirect measure of the relationship between the market liquidity condition and HFTs' trading flow. Based on the Kyle model, in a perfect market with full liquidity, the auto-correlation of stock excess return should be at zero levels, since market-makers fully adjust stock prices for providing liquidity by inferring the information component from the trading flow of informed traders and noise traders. Therefore, the magnitude of the stock return's auto-correlation level can be regarded as the illiquidity level in the stock market, deviating from the optimal scenario in the Kyle model. The regression formula for measuring HFTs' liquidity-timing style is as follows:

$$\tilde{R}^i_{t,t+60} = \alpha + \beta \tilde{R}^i_{t-60,t} + \gamma (Opposite\_Flow^i_{t-60,t} * \tilde{R}^i_{t-60,t}) + \kappa_i X_i + \varepsilon, \tag{10}$$

where the key term, $Opposite\_Flow^i_{t-60,t}$, is defined as:

$$Opposite\_Flow^i_{t-60,t} = \begin{cases} |HFT\_Flow^i_{t-60,t}|, & \text{if } HFT\_Flow^i_{t-60,t} * \tilde{R}^i_{t-60,t} < 0 \\ -|HFT\_Flow^i_{t-60,t}|, & \text{otherwise} \end{cases} \tag{11}$$

where *Opposite_Flow* represents HFTs' trading flow in the direction *opposite* to the direction of stock return at the same time. For example, if the stock return is positive during the past 60 seconds, then *Opposite_ Flow* is positive (negative) and HFTs execute a net short (long) trading flow during the past 60 seconds as well. In Eq. 10, the coefficient β is the primary measure for the illiquidity level of stocks, and the key coefficient of interest, γ, is the secondary measure for the co-movement of HFTs' flow with the stock illiquidity level. If γ is significant and holds the same sign as β, then it implies that HFTs exert their liquidity-timing skills by trading aggressively during times when the stock market is more illiquid.

Table 8 shows the regression results from Eq. 9. Similar to those in the previous subsection, each observation is measured at the beginning of each minute during the market hour, per stock per trading day, and all regression was done by randomly selecting four million stock-day-minute observations from the entire sample. By looking at Table 8, first it is clear to see that the excess return itself shows a significant negative auto-correlation pattern. From column (2), a 1% increase in the past 60-second excess return leads to a decrease of future 60-second excess return by 1.20 basis points. Comparing column (2) to column (4), we also find that the reversal pattern is stronger among large stocks, which again aligns with the argument that HFTs have a stronger incentive to trade in the opposite direction to the current return level (also shown in the previous subsection). Second, HFTs' net trading flow indeed has a positive prediction power on future stock return. The increase of HFTs' net trading flow by one standard deviation leads to the future increase of stock excess return by 0.8 basis points. This magnitude is consistent with the finding from Hendershott (2011) that HFTs' average return performance is around one basis point. Not surprisingly, we can also see that the positive predictive power of HFTs' trading flow on future return is more significant among large stocks.

Throughout all the regression results, the R^2 coefficients are very low and never go beyond 0.001. To explain this issue, Campbell & Thompson (2008) points out that whether the predictive regression is economically meaningful or not should depend on the comparison between R^2 and the square of the Sharpe Ratio (S^2) from the baseline model, rather than on the magnitude of R^2 alone. If R^2 has a comparable magnitude against S^2, then the extra prediction power of stock return from adding these factors should be considered economically significant. Indeed, in my regression setup, because each observation is measured only by minutes, the average minute-wise

Sharpe Ratio across stocks, which is the unconditional Sharpe Ratio of risky assets, is only 0.0001. Therefore, in order to quantify the enhancement of investment performance after taking extra factors into consideration, I applied the following adjustment factor from Campbell & Thompson (2008), which measures the proportional increase of the expected return from the baseline level after observing external factors, upon controlling the same magnitude of risk exposure, as:

$$\left(\frac{R^2}{1-R^2}\right)\left(\frac{1+S^2}{S^2}\right), \tag{12}$$

where S^2 measures the square of average unconditional Sharpe Ratio of risky assets, and R^2 is the coefficient of determination from each regressions after including different factors as regressors.

The results of all the adjustment factors are listed in the last row of Table 8, labelled as "Return increase (%)". Compared with the baseline strategy of merely holding stocks throughout the time, column (1) shows that adding the factor of past excess return increases the expected return level by 7.49%. After adding extra firm fixed effect in column (2), the increase of return further rises up to 75.65%, implying the importance of considering the heterogeneity of return reversal pattern across stocks when predicting future return. However, after adding the normalized HFT net flow as an additional factor, in column (3), we can see that the increase of return sharply rises to 299.75%, which is nearly four times greater than the figure that results from considering only past return and stock fixed effect as predictors. In columns (4) and (5), we can see that the increase of return is even more significant among large stocks (349.21%) and middle stocks (538.37%). Therefore, the large magnitude of return improvement shows that, after adjusting the low R^2 results caused by the short measuring period per observation, the prediction power of HFTs' net flow on future stock return is, indeed, of large economic magnitude.

[Insert Table 8 here.]

Table 9 tests HFTs' liquidity-timing style based on regression formula from Eq. 10. All other relevant setups for this regression test are similar to those in Table 8. By looking at the interaction term between HFTs' liquidity provision shares and stock excess return, we can see that all coefficients are significantly negative from column (3) to column (6): For example, when HFTs' net flow is in the opposite direction of contemporaneous stock excess return, stocks' return reversal pattern becomes even stronger in the future minute. From the adjustment factors listed in the last row of the table, including the interaction term leads to the increase of return jumping from 75.65% to 187.21%, which validates the idea that HFTs build up larger trading flow during times when the stock market is illiquid.

[Insert Table 9 here.]

In the last subsection, I showed that one of the important features behind HFTs' market-making trading style is its future net flow being opposite to past stock excess return; while for active-trading styles in this subsection, it's the HFTs' past net flow that predicts stocks' future return. Though these two styles have different motivations, it is still questionable whether the endogeneity issue of HFTs' net flow from past return may exist in these tests. For example, suppose HFTs' trading flow is purely driven by the market-making behavior based on stocks' past return level (as was shown previously in Table 3). Then, it is possible that the predictability of stock return in the speculative-trading test (Eq. 9) and the liquidity-timing test (Eq. 10) could be merely driven by the past return over a longer time horizon, rather than by HFTs actively executing net trading flow to profit from their trading skills. To clarify this potential endogeneity issue, I modified Eq. 9 and 10 by adding extra terms of stock return as regressors in order to cover all past excess return levels from $t - 3600$ to ts:

$$\tilde{R}^i_{t,t+60} = \alpha + \beta_0 \tilde{R}^i_{t-60,t} + \beta_1 \tilde{R}^i_{t-120,t-60} + \beta_2 \tilde{R}^i_{t-300,t-120} + \beta_3 \tilde{R}^i_{t-3600,t-300}$$
$$+ \phi HFT\_Flow^i_{t-60,t} + \kappa_i X_i + \varepsilon, \tag{13}$$

$$\tilde{R}^i_{t,t+60} = \alpha + \beta_0 \tilde{R}^i_{t-60,t} + \beta_1 \tilde{R}^i_{t-120,t-60} + \beta_2 \tilde{R}^i_{t-300,t-120} + \beta_3 \tilde{R}^i_{t-3600,t-300}$$
$$+ \gamma(Opposite\_Flow^i_{t-60,t} * \tilde{R}^i_{t-60,t}) + \kappa_i X_i + \varepsilon \tag{14}$$

Table 10 and 11 show robust testing results, based on Eq. 13 and 14 by controlling stocks' past return over a longer time span. In both tables, we can see that, although stocks' excess return still shows a negative auto-correlation pattern around 120 seconds, the coefficients for HFT_Flow and $Opposite\_Flow_{t-60,t}^{i} * \tilde{R}_{t-60,t}^{i}$ are still significant, and the increase of returns by adding these key terms are still large in magnitude. The increase of return rises from 99.79% to 360.10% after adding the term HFT_Flow in Table 10, and rises from 99.79% to 236.47% after adding the term $Opposite\_Flow_{t-60,t}^{i} * \tilde{R}_{t-60,t}^{i}$ in Table 11. By passing this robust test, I validate my original argument that HFTs generally adopt active-trading styles to enhance their profit level. In other words, HFTs' trading flows have an information component that reveals future stock price movement in the short term.

[Insert Table 10 here.]

[Insert Table 11 here.]

Before we move to the next chapter, it is important to re-emphasize the critical difference between HFTs' market-making and active-trading styles, as well as their market impact. HFTs mainly utilize market-making strategy to profit from market rebate and liquidity premium, and the entire security market benefits from the reduction of spread, implementation costs, and volatility, due to the intensified competition between HFTs and traditional market-makers. However, HFTs' also use active-trading strategies to skim profits from other market participants, which may increase the implementation costs and market volatility, and can even cause short-term severe price shifts since HFTs may aggressively take liquidity on one side of the order book. Based on these differences, there are two interesting questions that remain unsolved. First, are HFTs' different trading styles inter-connected with each other, in the sense that HFTs' active-trading activities affect their market-making incentives at the same time? Second, how do HFTs' trading styles, once news events hit the market, contribute to the price efficiency that reflects the stock market quality? In the next two chapters, I will try to provide some insights into these questions by examining

HFTs' trading styles during news events.

Chapter 4   Event study: Heterogeneity of HFTs' trading

styles across news events

In this chapter, I apply news events selected from RavenPack, to observe how HFTs' trading styles evolve after news information hits the market. My analysis focuses on two key points. First, what trading styles HFTs adopt when market events happen, and how these trading styles differ across different news event topics. Second, how different trading styles from HFTs affect the market quality, in terms of price discovery contribution and short-term volatility.

In the previous chapter, I showed that HFTs generally present two major types of trading styles, i.e., market-making and active-trading. The empirical strategies used to identify these styles are also employed in my event study in order to test HFTs' trading styles after events.

To be specific, I revised the empirical tests as follows. By uniformly setting the news arrival timestamp as $t = 0$, the following regression was used to measure HFTs' market-making trading style:

$$HFT\_Flow^i_{60,120} = \alpha + \beta \tilde{R}^i_{0,60} + \kappa_i X_i + \varepsilon, \tag{15}$$

and the following two regression formulas were utilized to measure HFTs' active-trading styles, speculative-trading and liquidity-timing:

$$\tilde{R}^i_{60,120} = \alpha + \beta \tilde{R}^i_{0,60} + \phi HFT\_Flow^i_{0,60} + \kappa_i X_i + \varepsilon, \tag{16}$$

$$\tilde{R}^i_{60,120} = \alpha + \beta \tilde{R}^i_{0,60} + \gamma(Opposite\_flow^i_{0,60} * \tilde{R}^i_{0,60}) + \kappa_i X_i + \varepsilon, \tag{17}$$

In all three regression formulas above, note that I mainly utilized the stock return and HFTs' trading flow within 0~60s after events, in order to predict the next 60-second stock return or HFTs' trading flow. The purpose of these designs was to measure how HFTs respond to the initial market reactions, after market investors start to absorb news information into price adjustments. As will be shown in later analysis, the speed at which stock prices fully adjust from events is relatively slow, implying market inefficiency that contrasts with the semi-strong market hypothesis. Therefore, HFTs' faster trading actions may potentially align with their motivation for seeking profit opportunities from this price-discovery process.

For each news topic group with more than 200 event observations in RavenPack (see Table 2 for news statistics across topics), I performed the regressions listed above on all events within each topic group, and recorded β from Eq. 15 representing HFTs' market-making style, ϕ from Eq. 16 representing HFTs' speculative-trading style, and γ from Eq. 17 representing HFTs' liquidity-timing style.

Table 12 presents the summary of all key regression coefficients under each news topic group. The first row "All topics" records the results when regression was performed among all 25,419 events from RavenPack. From this row, we can see that the signs of all three key coefficients ϕ, γ and β are the same as in the previous chapter, with the magnitude of ϕ and β being significantly larger than the results shown in the last chapter. These results imply that HFTs' market-making and active-trading styles still persist, and are possibly even stronger, around news events than they are during normal times. Furthermore, in the following rows of the table, the coefficients are reported by regression within each topic group, and all groups are sorted by the magnitude of ϕ generated by regression Eq. 16. From these results, we observe several interesting findings. First, it is clear that there is substantial heterogeneity across news topics in terms of the speculative-trading coefficients, ϕ. From the top eight news topics, such as "Acquisition-mergers", "Investor-relations", "Analyst-ratings", "Revenues" etc., regressions generate significantly positive ϕ with an average magnitude larger than 1.5; while among other news topics, regressions typically show insignificant or even negative ϕ. Second, the top eight news topics also generally have significant negative results on the liquidity-timing coefficient, γ, while none of the γs is significant from other news topics. Third, by looking at the market-making coefficient, β, we can see the patterns are shown in the opposite fashion: the significance of ϕ coefficients are only shown among the bottom five news topic groups, while ϕ coefficients from other new topics are typically not significant at all.

The results from Table 12 reflect important characteristics of HFTs' trading styles around news events. As I discussed in the previous chapter, the market-making coefficient β can be perceived to represent HFTs' function as liquidity-makers who increase the liquidity of the entire stock market and thus benefits non-HFTs, while ϕ and γ coefficients represent HFTs' ability to actively trade to skim profit from the market, which implicitly comes at the cost of other non-HFTs. When looking at the top eight topics in Table 12, we can realize that these topics typically have significant ϕ and γ, but without significant β. These patterns imply that HFTs have specific skills in predicting the future price movement trends from these news topics, and that they trade by leaning more towards active-trading activities but less towards market-making activities. On the other hand, among the bottom eight news topics, the ϕ and γ coefficients are typically insignificant, while β coefficients are significantly negative. These results imply that HFTs focus purely on market-making business, with no ability to profit from active-trading on these types of events. Therefore, HFTs' contribution to the market quality may also be widely different across news topics. Lastly, it is interesting to realize that, when looking back on the row "All topics", all parameters ϕ, γ, β are significant when all events are pooled together into regression. However, the significance of these coefficients turns out to be actually driven by different news events, as clearly seen by the regression results under each news topic. These results underscore the importance of realizing the contingency of HFTs' contribution to the overall market quality based on different types of news events, since HFTs' market-making and active-trading styles are shown to be strongly exclusive against each other in the test.

[Insert Table 12 here.]

To show the persistence of results provided in Table 12 throughout different time periods, in Table 13 and Table 14 I did robust checking via a two-fold validation test, by redoing all regressions within each different news topic, but within the years 2008 and 2009 separately. Results from these two tables show that all key regression coefficients are persistent between these two separate years, proving that my results did indeed capture HFTs' different trading styles across different news topics, rather than merely capturing noises due to limited event samples. To simplify news categories based on HFTs' corresponding trading styles, I separated news topics into two main subgroups: "Informative News" covering all news events under the top eight topics in Table 12 ("Acquisition-mergers", "Investor-relations", "Analyst-ratings", "Revenues", "Credit-ratings", "Earnings", "Insider-trading" and "Labor-issues"), and "Noisy News" covering all news events under the bottom eight topics in Table 12 ("Products-services", "Dividends", "Marketing",

"Legal", "Partnerships", "Technical-analysis", "Stock-prices" and "Equity-actions").

[Insert Table 13 here.]

[Insert Table 14 here.]

Since HFTs' trade flow has significant prediction power on future stock movement in the "Informative News" group, it is naturally intriguing to see whether HFTs indeed alter their trading patterns and how they impact stock volatility by comparing statistical patterns between the "Informative News" and "Noisy News" subgroups. To capture stock volatility in a short period, I applied Return Variation, as defined in Eq. 3, as the proxy for measuring short-term stock volatility. The statistics of Return Variation around news event time is presented in Table 15. In columns, $RV_{a,b}$ measures the Return Variation from time $t = a$ to time $t = b$. For quantifying the change of stock volatility, $Ratio_X$ is defined as $RV_{0,X}/RV_{-X,0}$. Therefore, a ratio larger than one implies stock volatility increases after events occur. In rows, for purposes of clarity, all news topics are sorted in the same order as in Table 12, where news topics in the "Informative News" group are listed at the top and topics in the "Noisy News" group are listed at the bottom.

First, looking at the row "No equity actions", we can see that, after removing 640 events from the last topic "Equity actions", whose return variation abnormally decreases after events, the other events in aggregate show increasing return variation after events. The return variation changed from 58.69 within 60 seconds before events to 70.10 within 60 seconds after events, an increase in volatility of 19% (shown in Column "Ratio_60s"). However, the increase in return variation is transient and quickly diminishes over time, shown by the decrease of the variation ratio from 1.19 in Column "Ratio_60s", to 1.10 in Column "Ratio_120s", then a final drop to 0.95 in Column "Ratio_300s". Second, by looking at the change of return variation within each topic, we can see that topics within the "Informative News" subgroup, in general, show an increase of return variation more significant than that from topics within the "Noisy News" subgroup. The average "Ratio_60s" within the "Informative News" subgroup is 1.23, much higher than the level of 0.97

from the "Noisy News" group events, after excluding all events within the topic "Equity-actions". Based on these findings, we can conclude that during news events, the increase of short-period stock volatility is mainly driven by HFTs' active-trading activities. Compared with previous literature, my results contrast with Hasbrouck & Saar (2013), showing that increased low-latency activity from HFTs improves traditional market quality measures, including lower short-term volatility, during periods with heightened economic uncertainty. To explain these differences, it is important to point out that Hasbrouck and Saar defined a specific trading style named a "strategic run" pattern, which is typically an alternating series of submissions, cancellations, and executions shown in the order feed data, as the proxy for HFTs' trading activities. However, the "strategic run" pattern may have the limit of only replicating HFTs' market-making styles, while ignoring the HFTs' active-trading style, which is usually executed by consistent, directional trading messages. In contrast, my study shows that the effect on market volatility may be highly dependent on HFTs' choice of trading styles. Therefore, my results again indicate the importance of having a comprehensive view of HFTs' trading styles before analyzing their impact on market quality.

[Insert Table 15 here.]

However, it is important to point out that Table 12 does not indicate a causal relationship between HFTs' trading activities and market volatility. It is possible that either it is HFTs' trades that cause market turbulence and increase stock volatility, or it is the increase of stock volatility, which may due to trading reactions from non-HFTs, that incentivize HFTs to perform more active trades, or it may be any combination of these two channels. One way to shed some light on this problem is to look at the evolution of trading volumes after event time, which is shown in Figure 10. Red lines (Blue lines) represent results for which liquidity-takers are HFTs (non-HFTs), and solid lines (dash lines) represent results from all events under the "Informative News" subgroup ("Noisy News" subgroup). From these tables, it is clear to see that, under the "Informative News" subgroup, for trades initiated by either HFTs or non-HFTs, both the levels of trading volumes and trading numbers peak at the very beginning after events, and then gradually decrease over the time. Therefore, Figure 10 shows that both HFTs and non-HFTs react to market news by immediately taking more liquidity, making it hard to identify the direction of causal relationship between HFTs' trading activities and stock volatility.

[Insert Figure 10 here.]

To summarize, I applied a news event study and found that, although HFTs' trading activities become more intensified after all news events, HFTs lean towards different trading styles depending on the news topic. and HFTs' active-trading style contributes more to stock price volatility. Moreover, these two trading style categories, "market-making" and "active-trading", are shown to be exclusive of one another. The reasons for this strong exclusive pattern between HFTs' two trading styles remain to be discovered by future studies, but one main reason may stem from the highly competitive nature of the HFT industry. When HFTs detect active-trading opportunities and take liquidity from the market, these actions imply that their limit orders will also likely be adversely selected by other HFT competitors. Therefore, HFTs' active-trading styles will be accompanied by a reduction of their market-making activities, leading to potential liquidity evaporation in the stock market (see Copeland & Galai (1983)). To verify this idea, future researchers should try to explore methods to identify different individual players *within* the HFT family, since this relevant feature is unfortunately missed in my current dataset.

Chapter 5   Analysis of HFTs' price discovery role from news events

This chapter utilizes the event study to analyze the price discovery process after news events. The unique feature of my dataset, which contains both real-time trading records identifying HFT players and exogenous news event information, enabled me to discover how trades initiated by different players facilitate price efficiency, by adjusting the stock price to the new equilibrium level after news events hit the market. Few papers cover this topic, among which the analysis is limited to showing that HFTs' trading flow aligns with the direction of the permanent stock price movement (see Brogaard, Hendershott & Riordan (2014)). My analysis in this chapter will enhance the depth of this topic by comparing the price discovery contribution between HFT and non-HFT players, from the perspectives of both trading speed and trading styles. I will also use these results to provide insight to policymakers who strive to improve the market quality via better policy design.

To quantify the attribution of cumulative price impact among different traders, I applied the identification strategy from Barclay & Warner (1993), who originally analyzed the relationship between price impact level and trading sizes during the periods before takeover announcements. For a trade k with execution price P_k, the price impact from this trade, named as I_k, is defined as:

$$I_k = P_k - P_{k-1}, \tag{18}$$

The price impact is measured as the change of the execution price level, from the last trade record to the current trade record. Next, in order to measure the cumulative price impact from trades initiated by different liquidity-takers, I defined the $CumPChange$ of trades, with liquidity-takers as HFTs (HX) or non-HFTs (NX), as the sum of the price impact among all trades with the same identity of liquidity-takers:

$$CumPChange_{HX} = \sum_{k \in HX} I_k, \quad CumPChange_{NX} = \sum_{k \in NX} I_k, \tag{19}$$

Therefore, given a specified period, the fraction of cumulative price change attributed to different liquidity-takers is defined as:

$$CumPChange\%_{HX} = CumPChange_{HX}/(CumPChange_{HX} + CumPChange_{NX}),$$

$$CumPChange\%_{HX} = CumPChange_{HX}/(CumPChange_{HX} + CumPChange_{NX}), \qquad (20)$$

Note that, by this definition, for each type of trades, the sign of cumulative price change fraction is based on the direction of the total price change aggregated from all trades. This means, when the overall shift in stock price is positive (negative), the fraction of cumulative price change from one specific type of trade will be positive only if the cumulative price change from these trades are positive (negative). Therefore, a greater positive level of cumulative price change indicates that trades contribute more in facilitating stock price to move to the new equilibrium level.

Before diving into the price discovery analysis on news events, it is important to examine how price discovery contributes to different types of trades throughout the entire sample period. There are two reasons for this step. First, it will check whether my results are still consistent with the main findings from Barclay & Warner (1993). Based on their analysis from 1981 to 1984, the middle-sized trades are the main driving force for stock price discovery, since informed traders intended to use large trades for faster execution but are not willing to make their trades too large for fear of revealing themselves to other market players. However, these results may have significantly changed over the past 20 years due to evolution of the market structure, trading technologies, etc. Second, the results measured from my entire sample period will be regarded as the benchmark to compare against later results in the event study, to clearly show how HFTs' trading style affects the level of price discovery contribution.

In Table 16, I calculated the attribution of cumulative price change among all 120 stocks, covering all trading days in the years 2008 to 2009. The "Trade", "Volume" and "CumPChange" columns calculate the fraction of the number of trading records, traded shares, and cumulative price change within each subgroup. Column "Before/At/After" corresponds to trading statistics before/at/after market hours, and Column "AllTime" corresponds to trading statistics throughout all periods. For rows, statistics are shown within each subgroup differing by the share for each trade (e.g., "≤100" means all trades with sizes no larger than 100 shares). Following Barclay & Warner (1993), rows "Small", "Middle" and "Large" summarize statistics among trades with sizes $\leq$ 500 shares, $>$500 & $\leq$10,000 shares, and $>$10,000 shares. Additionally, rows "HH", "HN", "NH" and "NN" calculate statistics among trades differing by the identities of liquidity-takers and liquidity-makers.

First, from looking at the trading statistics among different sizes of stocks in Table 16, I found that the results largely differ from Barclay & Warner (1993). Indeed, in 2008 to 2009, small trades account for 84.2% of total trade records, 32.6% of trading volume, and 90.2% of cumulative price change. All these numbers are much higher than the results from Barclay & Warner (1993), which showed that small trades accounting for 60.2% of trade records, 14.5% of trading volume, and 1.5% of cumulative price change. Various reasons can lead to these sharp differences over the past 30 years, including the change of structure within the U.S. stock market (decimalization and market fragmentation from the increase of U.S. exchange venues), market regulations (Regulation NMS Act in 2005), or even the entry of new types of traders such as HFTs. However, I suggest that the introduction of the automotive trading algorithm is the critical reason. Since the upgrade of trade execution strategies from automotive trading algorithms in 2005, informed traders can further conceal their trading motivation by truncating large size of orders into multiple tiny orders to execute, thus hiding their orders in the market flow and avoiding discovery of their trading incentive by other players. This reason may explain why the cumulative price change attributed from small trades changed significantly from only 1.5% from 1981~1984 to 90.2% from 2008~2009.

Next, by looking at the statistics across four different types of trades, we can see that HFTs account for large fraction of total trading activities in the stock market. Among all trades where HFTs are as liquidity-takers (summing up Row "HH" and "HN"), HFTs represent 47.9% of total trades and 38.2% of total volume. However, the attribution of cumulative price change from HFTs is relatively small, at only 10.1%, and these contributions are concentrated within market hours. These results imply two facts about HFTs' trading styles. First, since HFTs largely participate in the market-making business, their price discovery contribution may get offset between their ability to capture the short-term reversal pattern of stock price and their potential losses from being adversely selected by other liquidity-takers. Therefore, HFTs' market-making trading style, although a large contributor to the total number of trades and shares from HFTs, does not have a large net contribution on the price discovery process. Second, HFTs' active-trading activities are most likely to show up during market hours, since the emergence of more market information updates and trading flows enables HFTs to find more short-term profit opportunities from active-trading. Therefore, it leaves the possibility that HFTs' active-trading styles may facilitate the price discovery process, especially during times of massive information inflow, such as news event periods.

[Insert Table 16 here.]

Now we turn to the results from event studies. Table 17 provides the statistics for trades, volume, and cumulative price change within 0~300s after news events[4], with results aggregated under each different news topic group. Statistics are shown based on the identity of liquidity-takers, with "HX" representing trades whose liquidity-takers are HFTs, and "NX" representing trades whose liquidity-takers are non-HFTs. Again, for ease of comparison, news topics are sorted in the same order as in Table 12, with "Informative News" topics listed in the top rows and "Noisy News" topics listed in the bottom rows. By looking at the first two columns, we can see that the fraction of cumulative price change initiated by HFTs is generally around 30%, which is much higher than the level of 10% from the entire sample period (as shown in Table 16). Furthermore, the fraction of cumulative price change among all "Informative News" topics is 36.3%, which is also much higher than the average level from "Noisy News" topics (28.0%). To rule out the possibility that these differences are driven by trading frequency or volume, I also listed the fraction of trading volume or trading records initiated by HFTs. In columns "HX_Volume" and "HX_Trades", there is no significant difference in the fraction of trading volume or number of trades between the "Informative News" and "Noisy News" groups. Due to difference of HFTs' trading styles between the "Informative News" and "Noisy News" subgroups, my results imply that it is HFTs' active-trading styles that facilitate the price discovery process more after news events.

[Insert Table 17 here.]

---

[4]Due to the price persistency pattern during events, I selected $0 \sim 300s$ as the time window for event study. Table 18 validates this idea, by showing that the price movement pattern is persistent within the first 300 seconds after events. After events occur, stock return from first 30 seconds has a strong correlation with the 30~300s stock return, but the correlation is diminished when the return is further measured within 300~900s. Furthermore, it is also observable that the price persistency pattern is stronger among news topics in the "Informative News" group.

To further discover the relationship between HFTs' incentives behind the active-trading styles and their price discovery contribution, Figure 3 shows the evolution of cumulative price change across different liquidity-takers and different types of news events. The X-axis represents the cumulative time (in seconds) after news events happened, and the Y-axis, "cumulative price change", represents the average cumulative price changes (in dollar value) under each type of trades, with the sign aligning with the direction of 300-second cumulative total price changes[5]. Solid lines represent results from all events under the "Informative News" subgroup, and dashed lines represent results from all events under the "Noisy News" subgroup. Within the "Informative News" subgroup, by comparing the cumulative price change between "HX" trades (in blue lines) and "NX" trades (in red lines), I made several findings. First, at the very beginning of "Informative News" events, HX trades tend to have a larger contribution to cumulative price change than do NX trades. Second, starting from around 100 seconds after events, the curve of cumulative price change for HX trades becomes almost flat, implying HFTs' liquidity-taking actions do not further facilitate price discovery during this period. However, for NX trades, the cumulative price impact shows a consistently increasing pattern, within the entire 300 seconds after market events happen. These distinct patterns indicate that the heterogeneity of news reaction speeds among different players after news events occur due to HFTs' active-trading behavior: at the very beginning after news events hit the market, HFTs tend to react faster than non-HFTs by taking liquidity in the same direction as the permanent price change. On the contrary, non-HFTs respond much more slowly to these events. Figure 3 shows that liquidity-taking trades from non-HFTs continue driving the price to the new equilibrium, even after HFTs stop contributing to price discovery. These different patterns between HFTs and non-HFTs may have several explanations: HFTs may be more professional in interpreting and trading on news information, or non-HFTs may pay limited attention and fail to notice news events instantly. A further plausible reason could be that HFTs trade on news events faster than non-HFTs, on average, but slower than the fastest non-HFTs. After news events, HFTs can detect market order flows from the fastest-reacting non-HFTs, and HFTs thus follow the trading directions led by non-HFTs. Based on this strategy, HFTs (and possibly the

---

[5]For example, if the 300-second stock price change after events is positive (negative), then the "cumulative price change" would be positive if the total price changes caused by one type of trades is positive (negative). Essentially, a positive Y-value means the trades contribute in moving stock price in the same direction towards the price level at 300 seconds after the events.

fastest-reacting non-HFTs) skim profit from other slower-reacting non-HFTs, who start trading and pushing price further only after HFTs have already built up their active-trading positions. In short, this "event momentum" pattern, caused by the various reaction speeds across non-HFTs, incentivizes HFTs to initiate a speculative-trading style and profit from market events. Lastly, it is important to point out that my empirical finding does not overlap with the traditional view that HFTs play a "winner-takes-all" game by reducing trading latency in the magnitude of milliseconds, when reacting to news announcements (see Scholtus, van Dijk & Frijns (2014), Foucault, Kadan & Kandel (2013) and Hendershott & Riordan (2012)). Rather, my results show that the profit opportunity for HFTs is due to the "limited attention" characteristic of non-HFT players, since the time window for seizing profits after events lasts over tens of seconds rather than merely milliseconds, an idea that has not been covered in previous literature.

[Insert Figure 3 here.]

However, one restriction from the empirical design in Figure 3 is that the identities of liquidity-makers are neglected in the analysis, which leaves the possibility that HFTs profit from liquidity-taking trades but may also lose significantly from liquidity-making trades. To prove HFTs generate profits from their trading activities, Figure 4 plots HFTs' cumulative inventory level around news event times. The calculation of HFTs' inventory is based on Eq. 2 by aggregating HFTs' net trading flow during the period around news events[6]. Due to the large heterogeneity of HFTs' trading volume across different stocks, HFTs' inventory is again normalized by the average minute-wise volume for each stock, based on the trading volume during the past five calendar days before events. For comparison purposes, I set the HFT cumulative inventory to zero at $t = 0$ in Figure 4. Based on the plot, we can find that HFTs' inventory is generally stable before news events; however, after news events, HFTs' inventory sharply increases during the first 30 seconds, with the cumulative inventory level being more than 60% of the minute-wise trading volume, or around 800 shares per event, on average. Afterward, HFTs' inventory shows a generally decreasing pattern and becomes stable after 200 seconds, with the stabled net inventory level even being slightly negative,

---

[6]Again, the sign of cumulative inventory is positive if the inventory position aligns with the direction of 300-second stock price changes. Otherwise, the sign for the inventory position would be negative.

compared to the level at $t = 0$. Combined with the results from Figure 3, we can see the strong relationship between HFTs' net inventory level and their price discovery contribution: within 0~50s after news events, the sharp increase of HFTs' net inventory level accompanies more than 60% of total cumulative price changes from HFT-initiated trades; while after the first 50 seconds, when HFTs start reverting their positions to zero levels, the additional cumulative price change amount from HFTs gets reduced immediately. Therefore, Figure 4 effectively aligns HFTs' active-trading strategy with their price discovery contribution.

[Insert Figure 4 here.]

From Barclay & Warner (1993), the incentive for informed traders to execute middle-sized trades is to enable trades that are large enough to build up positions quickly, but not so large as to be noticed by other players. While in the current U.S. stock market, as trading sizes becoming much smaller due to the availability of automated trading techniques for all traders (as shown from Table 16), the trading patterns for informed-trading activities changed correspondingly. In my event study, due to the main finding that HFTs facilitate price discovery by taking fast active-trading strategies, the next questions are how do HFTs execute these strategies, and whether their trading pattern is distinguishable from that of non-HFTs. To answer these questions, in Figure 5 and Figure 6, I further plot the distribution of trading frequency and average trading size across all events within the "Informative News" group. In both figures, each stacked bar shows the percentage distribution of the number of trades (or average sizes), under each 10-second time window aggregated from all events. For example, the bar labeled with "0_10s" represents the distribution of the number of trades within 0~10s after event timestamp. Different colors show the percentage of events within different subgroups. Figure (a) shows the distribution when the liquidity-takers are HFTs (HX), and Figure (b) shows the distribution when the liquidity-takers are non-HFTs (NX).

From Figure 5, it is clear that the trade number distribution shows a shifting pattern for both HX and NX Trades, while the trend is more significant among HX trades. For example, in Figure (a), the fraction of events with more than four HX trades between 0 and 10 seconds after event time is around 50%, while this number quickly decreases to 41% between 10 and 20 seconds, and finally decreases to 37% between 90 and 100 seconds. In Figure (b), the results are quite similar for NX trades, except that between 0 and 10 seconds, the fraction of events with more then four NX trades is smaller at 42%. At the same time, Figure 6 shows that the distribution pattern of average trading size across events is persistent throughout the time after news events, for both HX and NX trades. Based on the results from these two figures, we can see that, after news events, both HFT and non-HFT players execute their informed trading strategies by increasing their trading frequency rather than by increasing the average trading size level. These results reflect the fact that automated trading algorithms help traders to conceal their trading incentives by executing their trading orders more frequently, in small pieces, over time.

[Insert Figure 5 here.]

[Insert Figure 6 here.]

The last test I am interested in implementing examines how regulatory policies, such as the short-sale restriction, affect the price discovery process from both HFTs and non-HFTs. Though short sales are allowed for both HFTs and non-HFTs in regular time, it is commonly perceived that HFTs short-sale stocks more frequently than non-HFTs. The main reason is that HFTs generally have stringent restrictions on their risk exposure, keeping their trading positions small and their cumulative inventory levels around zero. Therefore, when negative news information comes into the stock market, HFTs are incentivized to change their net positions from zero to a negative level by short-selling stocks immediately. Therefore, short-sale restrictions should affect HFTs' trading behavior more, and thus HFTs' price discovery role, especially when stock prices are declining during the short-sale restriction period.

From September 18th to October 12nd, 2008, SEC took an temporary emergency action to prohibit short-sale activities in U.S. financial stocks, to "protect the integrity and quality of the securities market and strengthen investor confidence" during the financial crisis period. From previous research, the temporary short-sale ban also brought detrimental effect on nationwide market quality, such as reducing liquidity and deteriorating price support (see Boehmer, Jones & Zhang (2013), Beber & Pagano (2013), and Grundy, Lim & Verwijmeren (2012)). In terms of HFTs' contribution in market quality during the extremely volatile short-sale ban period, Brogaard, Hendershott & Riordan (2017) compared the heterogeneous impact of reducing HFTs' short-sale activities across different sizes of stocks, and they concluded that HFTs' activities are harmful to market liquidity by increasing the bid-ask spread. However, none of these studies provided concrete measures to effectively attribute the deterioration of market quality between HFT and non-HFT players. In my analysis, I aim to provide these answers, by comparing HFTs' and non-HFTs' contribution to the price discovery process within the policy restriction period.

Among all news events in my sample, 11,031 "Informative News" events are relevant to financial stocks throughout the entire sample period from 2008 to 2009, among which 532 events occurred during the short-sale restriction period. These sub-samples provide the opportunity to test how the price discovery process changed due to the restriction on short-selling activities for both HFTs and non-HFTs.

Figure 7 shows the evolution of cumulative price change from various sub-samples. All plots are made under the same logic as the one shown in Figure 3, but differ in the criteria of selecting events. First, I only use all events in the "Informative News" subgroup (17,324 events). Second, Figure (a) shows results only among financial stocks within the entire sample period (11,031 events), and Figure (b) shows results only among financial stocks in the time period of the SEC short-sale ban period (532 events). Third, in both Figures (a) and (b), solid lines represent events where the $0 \sim 300s$ stock price change is positive (227 events), and dashed lines represent events where the $0 \sim 300s$ stock price change is negative (282 events).

Looking at Figure (a), we can see that, throughout the entire sample period, the magnitude of price change is more significant, on average, when stock prices rise: The average change of stock prices is 0.293 dollars when stock prices increase after news events, and 0.134 dollars when stock prices decrease after events. Next, by comparing the price evolution process between HX and NX trades, we can see that HX trades still account for a more substantial fraction of price changes within 100s after news events, though the pattern seems more significant during events where stock price goes up. However, the patterns get significantly changed during the short-sale restriction period. In Figure (b), among events where stock price went down, the price discovery role for HX trades (blue dashed line) gets significantly reduced. The 300-second cumulative price change from HFT-initiated trades is only 0.014 dollars per event, which is much lower than the level of 0.050 dollars from the entire sample period (see Figure (a)). Additionally, we can see that the cumulative price change within $0 \sim 100$s after events becomes around zero dollars when stock prices go down, but the price discovery pattern is unchanged for HFTs among events when stock prices go up. For non-HFTs-initiated trades, the evolution of cumulative price change does not get significantly changed during the short-sale restriction period[7]. Among all above, the SEC's short-sale restriction seems only to have affected the price discovery function among HFTs' liquidity-taking trades, which effectively validates my argument that short-sale restrictions limit HFTs from executing their active-trading strategies, by preventing HFTs from instantly building up short positions via short-selling stocks mentioned in news events. Considering the wide range of previous studies criticizing the negative impact of the short-sale restriction ban on market quality, my analysis points out that these findings are mainly from the regulatory impact on HFTs' active-trading activities.

[Insert Figure 7 here.]

To conclude, in this chapter I investigated how HFTs contribute to the price discovery process from the process, in which all market players trade on news events and adjust stock prices to new equilibrium levels. HFT-initiated trades play a major role in facilitating price discovery in the early seconds after news events, but then the price discovery process is driven by non-HFT-initiated trades afterwards. This pattern aligns with HFTs' active-trading styles, in which HFTs quickly build up large net positions after events, and thereby skim profits from slow-reacting non-HFTs. From the perspective of regulatory policy, a short-sale restriction may help stabilize the market

---

[7]Note that non-HFTs' selling activities, represented by NX trades, lead to larger cumulative price changes during the short-sale ban period. However, the total absolute level of price changes after negative news, combining both HX and NX trades, are not significantly different between regular period and short-sale ban period. This indicates that the aggregate level of price impact from news are persistent between the regular period and the short-sale ban period. Result shows that HX trades almost contribute zero levels of price changes, and therefore all the price discovery contributions are loaded to NX trades. In fact, this implies that the short-sale ban effectively limited HFTs skimming profits from non-HFTs.

from during excessive short-term turbulence; however, this action would also deteriorate market price efficiency, because the restriction could effectively limit HFTs' active-trading strategy and their price discovery function.

Chapter 6   Conclusion

The primary objective of this paper is to investigate HFTs' different trading styles, how these trading styles are contingent on market conditions, and their consequent impact on the quality of the U.S. stock market. Based on theoretical predictions from previous literature, I validated the idea that HFTs show both market-making and active-trading styles, based on the real-time trading records. Moreover, the study showed that HFTs' market-making activities are disincentivized in times of higher stock volatility. These results provide empirical evidence supporting the characteristics of liquidity-provision activities from Kyle (1985) and Drechsler, Moreira & Savov (2018).

In addition, my event study shows that HFTs' trading styles are heterogeneous among different news events: when news information grants HFTs prediction power on the future stock price trends, HFTs lean towards active-trading style and away from market-making style. Otherwise, HFTs would merely focus on market-making business and pause active trading. Therefore, HFTs' market impact highly depends upon their trading incentives under different market conditions. These findings shed light on reconciling controversial arguments about HFTs' contribution to market quality (See Menkveld (2013), Hagströmer & Nordén (2013), Brogaard, Hendershott & Riordan (2014), Jovanovic & Menkveld (2016), and Boehmer, Fong & Wu (2018))

More importantly, the study also highlighted the importance of understanding HFTs' trading incentives before unveiling their market impact, based on two different aspects of the event study. First, I found that HFTs' active-trading style facilitates the price discovery process, due to HFTs' incentive for skimming profit from non-HFTs. The results are similar to the predatory trading pattern in Brunnermeier & Pedersen (2005). Second, the SEC's short-sale ban in 2008 effectively restricted HFTs' active-trading styles during the market downturn period, but at the cost of sacrificing HFTs' contribution on price discovery. One main takeaway from these results is that policymakers should deliberate market policy design, since banning specific trading activities may lead to the unexpected consequences of reducing market quality.

However, several questions are still left to be explored in later studies. First, how are trading styles inter-connected across different HFT firms? For example, are HFTs' trading styles independent of each other, or do late-responding HFTs firms chase after patterns from fast-responding

HFT firms? Second, how do HFTs extract the information component from news events? Do they "read" news by utilizing specific computer algorithms to generate faster trading responses than non-HFTs, or do they chase after the trading flow created by fast-reacting non-HFTs? Third, how do HFTs determine the level and holding period of active-trading positions after news events, in order to balance the trade-off between skimming profits and taking excessive risk exposure? Answering these questions would lead to a better understanding of HFTs' trading incentives, and bring deeper insight to market regulators and researchers for policy-design purposes, in order to utilize HFTs' trading styles to further enhance the quality of stock markets.

Bibliography

[1] Albert J. Menkveld, (2013), *High frequency trading and the new-market makers*, Journal of Financial Markets, 16, p. 712–40.

[2] Albert S. Kyle, (1985), *Continuous Auctions and Insider Trading.* Econometrica, vol. 53(6), p. 1315-1335.

[3] Alessandro Beber, Marco Pagano, (2013), *Short-Selling Bans Around the World: Evidence from the 2007–09 Crisis*, Journal of Finance, 68, issue 1, p. 343-381.

[4] Bruno Biais, Thierry Foucault and Sophie Moinas, *Equilibrium fast trading*, Journal of Financial Economics, vol. 116, issue 2, 292-313

[5] Björn Hagströmer, Lars Nordén, (2013), *The diversity of high-frequency traders*, Journal of Financial Markets, 16, p. 741–70.

[6] Boyan Jovanovic, Albert J. Menkveld, (2016), *Middlemen in limit-order markets*, Working Paper, New York University.

[7] Brogaard et al., (2016), *High-frequency trading and extreme price movements*, Working paper, University of Washington.

[8] Bruce D. Grundy, Bryan Lim, Patrick Verwijmeren, (2012), *Do option markets undo restrictions on short sales? Evidence from the 2008 short-sale ban*, Journal of Financial Economics, 106, issue 2, p. 331-348.

[9] Bruno Biais, Pierre Hillion, Chester Spatt, (1995), *An Empirical Analysis of the Limit Order Book and the Order Flow in the Paris Bourse*, Journal of Finance, 50, issue 5, p. 1655-89.

[10] Bruno Biais, Thierry Foucault, (2014), *HFT and Market Quality*, Bankers, Markets & Investors, 128, 5-19.

[11] Eric Budish, Peter Cramton, John Shim, (2015), *The High-Frequency Trading Arms Race: Frequent Batch Auctions as a Market Design Response*, The Quarterly Journal of Economics, vol. 130, issue 4, 1547-1621

[12] Chaboud et al., (2014), *Rise of the Machines: Algorithmic Trading in the Foreign Exchange Market*, The Journal of Finance, 69, p. 2045-2084.

[13] Chakravarty et al., (2012), *Clean Sweep: Informed Trading through Intermarket Sweep Orders*, The Journal of Financial and Quantitative Analysis, vol. 47, no. 2, p. 415–435

[14] Ekkehart Boehmer, Charles M. Jones, Xiaoyan Zhang, (2013), *Shackling Short Sellers: The 2008 Shorting Ban*, Review of Financial Studies, 26, issue 6, p. 1363-1400.

[15] Ekkehart Boehmer, Kingsley Y. L. Fong, Julie Wu, (2018), *Algorithmic Trading and Market Quality: International Evidence*, AFA 2013 San Diego Meetings Paper.

[16] Eugene F. Fama, Kenneth R. French, (1988), *Dividend yields and expected stock returns*, Journal of Financial Economics, 22, issue 1, p. 3-25.

[17] Itamar Drechsler, Alan Moreira, Alexi Savov, (2018), *Liquidity Creation As Volatility Risk*, working paper.

[18] Jean-Edouard Colliard, Thierry Foucault, (2012), *Trading Fees and Efficiency in Limit Order Markets*, Review of Financial Studies, 25, issue 11, p. 3389-3421.

[19] Jérôme Dugast, Thierry Foucault, (2018), *Data abundance and asset price informativeness*, Journal of Financial Economics, 130, issue 2, p. 367-391.

[20] Joel Hasbrouck, Gideon Saar, (2013), *Low-latency trading*, Journal of Financial Markets, 16, issue 4, p. 646-679.

[21] John Campbell, Samuel P. Thompson, (2008), *Predicting Excess Stock Returns Out of Sample: Can Anything Beat the Historical Average?*, Review of Financial Studies, 21, issue 4, p. 1509–1531.

[22] Jonathan Brogaard, Björn Hagströmer, Lars Nordén, Ryan Riordan, (2015), *Trading Fast and Slow: Colocation and Liquidity*, Review of Financial Studies, 28, issue 12, p. 3407-3443.

[23] Jonathan Brogaard, Terrence Hendershott, Ryan Riordan, (2014), *High-Frequency Trading and Price Discovery*, Review of Financial Studies, 27, issue 8, p. 2267-2306.

[24] Jonathan Brogaard, Terrence Hendershott, Ryan Riordan, (2017), *High frequency trading and the 2008 short-sale ban*, Journal of Finance, 124, issue 1, p. 22-42.

[25] Kirilenko et al., (2017), *The Flash Crash: the Impact of HFT on an Electronic Market*, Journal of Finance, Forthcoming.

[26] Liyan Yang, Haoxiang Zhu, (2018), *Back-Running: Seeking and Hiding Fundamental Information in Order Flows*, Working paper, Rotman School of Management.

[27] Markus K. Brunnermeier, Lasse Heje Pedersen, (2005), *Predatory Trading*, Journal of Finance, vol. 60(4), p. 1825-1863.

[28] Martin Scholtus, Dick van Dijk, Bart Frijns, (2014), *Speed, algorithmic trading, and market quality around macroeconomic news announcements*, Journal of Banking & Finance, 38, issue C, p. 89-105.

[29] Matthew Baron, Jonathan Brogaard, Andrei Kirilenko (2014), *The Trading Profits of High-Frequency Traders*, Working Paper, University of Washington.

[30] Matthew Baron, Jonathan Brogaard, Björn Hagströmer and Andrei Kirilenko, (2018), *Risk and Return in High-Frequency Trading*, Journal of Financial and Quantitative Analysis,e 54(3), 993-1024.

[31] Maureen O'Hara, Mao Ye, (2011), *Is market fragmentation harming market quality?*, Journal of Financial Economics, 100, issue 3, p. 459-474.

[32] Michael J. Barclay, Jerold B. Warner, (1993), *Stealth trading and volatility: Which trades move prices?*, Journal of Financial Economics, 34, issue 3, p. 281-305.

[33] Nicholas Hirschey, (2014), *Do High-Frequency Traders Anticipate Buying and Selling Pressure?*, Working paper, London Business School.

[34] Paul Tetlock, (2007), *Giving Content to Investor Sentiment: The Role of Media in the Stock Market*, Journal of Finance, Vol. 62, No. 3, 2007, p. 1139-1168.

[35] Robert A. Korajczyk, Dermot Murphy, (2019), *High-Frequency Market Making to Large Institutional Trades*, Review of Financial Studies, 32, issue 3, p. 1034–1067.

[36] Terrence Hendershott, (2011), *HFT and Price Efficiency*, Foresight Driver Review (DR12).

[37] Terrence Hendershott, Charles M. Jones, Albert Menkveld, (2011), *Does Algorithmic Trading Improve Liquidity?*, Journal of Finance, 66, issue 1, p. 1-33.

[38] Terrence Hendershott, Ryan Riordan, (2012), *Algorithmic Trading and the Market for Liquidity*, Journal of Financial and Quantitative Analysis, Vol. 48, No. 4, p. 1001–1024

[39] Thierry Foucault, Ohad Kadan, Eugene Kandel, (2013), *Liquidity Cycles and Make/Take Fees in Electronic Markets*, Journal of Finance, 68 (1), p. 299-341.

[40] Thomas E. Copeland, Dan Galai, (1983), *Information Effects on the Bid-Ask Spread*, Journal of Finance, 38, issue 5, p. 1457-69.

[41] Vincent van Kervel, Albert J. Menkveld, (2018), *High-Frequency Trading around Large Institutional Orders*, Journal of Finance, Forthcoming.

Table 1. Summary statistics for NASDAQ HFT Trading Dataset. All records are shown by average level per stock per day. All trade records are sub-grouped into columns by the trade types ("All", "HH", "HN", "NH" and "NN") and rows by the size of stocks measured by market capitalization ("All", "Large", "Middle" and "Small"). "Trades" represents the number of trading records, "Shares" represents trading shares (in thousands), and "Dollar" represents dollar volume traded (in millions).

		All	**HH**	**HN**	**NH**	**NN**
All Stocks	Trades	4,664.25	841.61	1,390.90	1,061.47	1,370.27
	Shares(,000)	1,759.35	284.83	386.81	584.26	503.46
	Dollar(M)	65.53	10.12	17.34	17.83	20.24
Large Stocks	Trades	11,929.13	2,358.91	3,550.39	2,908.18	3,111.65
	Shares(,000)	4,898.47	829.31	1,063.92	1,688.24	1,317.00
	Dollar(M)	188.73	29.92	49.73	52.44	56.65
Middle Stocks	Trades	1,596.78	150.62	520.89	229.64	695.63
	Shares(,000)	302.88	22.58	81.45	55.97	142.87
	Dollar(M)	6.62	0.39	2.01	0.90	3.32
Small Stocks	Trades	453.06	12.59	97.18	43.27	300.01
	Shares(,000)	71.19	1.65	13.84	6.68	49.01
	Dollar(M)	1.03	0.03	0.23	0.09	0.68

Table 1: Summary Statistics from NASDAQ HFT Dataset

Table 2. Statistics of news information extracted from RavenPack database. News events are filtered under the following criteria: 1. The NAME_ENTITY variable labels firm names that are in one of the 120 stocks in HFT Dataset; 2. News Date is between 01/01/2008 to 12/31/2009; 3. News timestamp (in EST Time) is between 9:30 a.m. to 4:00 p.m. (to ensure news happens during the market hour); 4. RELEVANCE$\geq$75 (to ensure news is relevant with target stock); 5. and G_ENS $= 100$ (to ensure no stale news exist); In total there are 25,419 news events selected from the database. News topics are listed in rows, based on the variable "Group" assigned for each event in RavenPack. The sentimental directions of news are listed in columns, which are "positive news" (with CSS>50), "negative news" (with CSS<50) or "neutral news" (with CSS=50). For simplicity, only the top 20 news types with the highest number of news observations are listed in this table.

	Total	Positive news	Negative news	Neutral news
insider-trading	5112	125	1662	3325
products-services	3762	1590	293	1879
earnings	3755	1222	863	1670
revenues	2724	1103	663	958
labor-issues	1577	568	294	715
acquisitions-mergers	1412	866	76	470
analyst-ratings	1244	548	404	292
credit-ratings	1045	204	383	458
stock-prices	710	329	288	93
legal	676	172	168	336
technical-analysis	646	278	72	296
equity-actions	640	136	177	327
partnerships	640	342	22	276
investor-relations	455	146	0	309
assets	344	80	55	209
dividends	290	249	21	20
marketing	226	67	10	149
regulatory	103	24	22	57
price-targets	46	31	11	4
Total	**25419**	**8084**	**5485**	**11850**

Table 2: Summary Statistics of selected news from RavenPack

Table 3. Dependency of HFTs' net trading flow on past return and volatility. Regressions are based on observations measured at the beginning of every minute during the market hours of NASDAQ, within each trading day and each available stocks in NASDAQ HFT Dataset. Columns (1) to (4) is based on Eq. 1, and columns (5) to (8) is based on Eq. 4 in the paper. Column (1) and (5) use observations from all stocks, while other columns only use observations among 40 large/middle/small stocks. For computation purpose, all regressions are done by randomly selecting four million stock-day-minute observations from the entire sample.

	(1) All Stocks	(2) Large Stocks	(3) Middle Stocks	(4) Small Stocks	(5) All Stocks	(6) Large Stocks	(7) Middle Stocks	(8) Small Stocks
Intercept	-0.000	-0.000	0.000	-0.001	0.000	-0.000	0.001**	-0.001
	(-0.733)	(-0.800)	(0.462)	(-0.947)	(0.952)	(-0.421)	(2.262)	(-0.956)
$\tilde{R}^i_{t-60,t}$	-2.678***	-4.862***	-3.984***	-2.241***	-1.701***	-2.379***	-3.834***	-2.230***
	(-12.621)	(-9.310)	(-11.773)	(-4.858)	(-5.374)	(-6.966)	(-7.047)	(-2.421)
$RV^i_{t-300,t}$	0.539	0.384	0.773	0.322	0.045	0.537	0.121	0.493
	(1.164)	(0.736)	(0.956)	(0.364)	(0.229)	(1.048)	(0.613)	(0.583)
$RV^{MKT}_{t-300,t}$	1.382	1.090	-0.327	3.526	0.045	0.537	0.121**	0.493
	(1.102)	(1.026)	(-0.163)	(1.166)	(-0.593)	(0.320)	(-2.178)	(1.143)
$RV^i_{t-300,t} * \tilde{R}^i_{t-60,t}$	47.247***	116.385***	60.079**	46.051**				
	(2.884)	(4.154)	(2.139)	(2.066)				
$RV^{MKT}_{t-300,t} * \tilde{R}^i_{t-60,t}$	2492.835***	4488.304***	3706.735***	2094.305***				
	(12.600)	(13.035)	(11.700)	(4.863)				
$\tilde{R}^i_{t-60,t}(\text{Middle } RV^i_{t-300,t},*)$					0.247**	0.397**	0.260	0.032
					(2.235)	(2.955)	(1.252)	(0.391)
$\tilde{R}^i_{t-60,t}(\text{High } RV^i_{t-300,t},*)$					0.438***	0.645***	0.725***	0.070
					(3.608)	(3.497)	(3.811)	(0.223)
$\tilde{R}^i_{t-60,t}(\text{Middle } RV^{MKT}_{t-300,t},*)$					0.698*	0.983**	0.496	1.005
					(1.754)	(2.321)	(0.746)	(0.843)
$\tilde{R}^i_{t-60,t}(\text{High } RV^{MKT}_{t-300,t},*)$					1.674***	2.376***	3.814***	2.252***
					(5.324)	(6.969)	(7.049)	(2.451)
Firm Fixed Effect	Yes	Yes	Yes	Yes	Yes	Yes	Yes	Yes
Month Fixed Effect	No	No	No	No	No	No	No	No
N	4000000	4000000	4000000	4000000	4000000	4000000	4000000	4000000
R2	0.002	0.003	0.005	0.001	0.001	0.003	0.004	0.001

Table 3: Dependency of HFTs' net trading flow on past return and volatility

Table 4. Robust test: Dependency of HFTs' trading flow on past return and volatility. All regression designs are the same as in Table 3, except replacing the dependent variable in Eq. 1 and Eq. 4 from $HFT\_Flow^i_{t,t+60}$ to $HFT\_Flow^i_{t-60,t}$, in order to measure how HFTs' trading flows are affected by simultaneous market conditions. Results are consistent with the findings in Table 3, except with the significance of regression results being stronger.

	(1) All Stocks	(2) Large Stocks	(3) Middle Stocks	(4) Small Stocks	(5) All Stocks	(6) Large Stocks	(7) Middle Stocks	(8) Small Stocks
Intercept	0.000	-0.001***	0.001	0.001	-0.000	-0.001**	0.001	-0.001
	(0.337)	(-2.679)	(1.482)	(0.839)	(-0.847)	(-2.062)	(1.239)	(-0.507)
$\tilde{R}^i_{t-60,t}$	-11.285***	-12.090***	-6.435***	-8.813***	-10.250***	-14.421***	-8.634***	-9.385***
	(-36.801)	(-27.324)	(-10.972)	(-13.730)	(-23.769)	(-29.798)	(-11.376)	(-11.336)
$RV^i_{t-300,t}$	2.156*	-0.811	1.519	2.571	1.756	-0.228	1.629	2.062
	(1.691)	(-0.552)	(0.692)	(1.071)	(1.428)	(-0.154)	(0.737)	(0.910)
$RV^{MKT}_{t-300,t}$	-2.830	3.841	-3.112	-6.468	1.756	-0.228	1.629	2.062
	(-0.813)	(1.281)	(-0.750)	(-0.776)	(-0.593)	(1.010)	(-0.711)	(-0.477)
$RV^i_{t-300,t} * \tilde{R}^i_{t-60,t}$	235.596***	355.513***	208.937**	86.818				
	(6.211)	(2.989)	(2.273)	(1.380)				
$RV^{MKT}_{t-300,t} * \tilde{R}^i_{t-60,t}$	10319.660***	11003.543***	2625.810***	8093.674***				
	(36.596)	(27.496)	(10.940)	(13.585)				
$\tilde{R}^i_{t-60,t}(Middle\ RV^i_{t-300,t})$					0.692***	0.846***	0.565***	0.373
					(7.398)	(9.874)	(4.157)	(1.159)
$\tilde{R}^i_{t-60,t}(High\ RV^i_{t-300,t})$					0.733***	1.042***	1.105***	0.160
					(8.319)	(12.342)	(8.556)	(0.698)
$\tilde{R}^i_{t-60,t}(Middle\ RV^{MKT}_{t-300,t})$					4.635***	5.316***	0.907	6.637***
					(8.519)	(8.864)	(0.965)	(6.315)
$\tilde{R}^i_{t-60,t}(High\ RV^{MKT}_{t-300,t})$					10.165***	14.380***	8.513***	9.373***
					(23.773)	(29.861)	(11.276)	(11.455)
Firm Fixed Effect	Yes	Yes	Yes	Yes	Yes	Yes	Yes	Yes
Month Fixed Effect	No	No	No	No	No	No	No	No
N	4000000	4000000	4000000	4000000	4000000	4000000	4000000	4000000
R-Square	0.017	0.027	0.004	0.008	0.010	0.018	0.005	0.006

Table 4: Dependency of HFTs' trading flow on past return and volatility (robust test)

Table 5. Regression of HFT portfolio on volatility shock level. Regression formula is based on Eq. 6. The HFT high-minus-low (HML) portfolio is constructed by ranking the past-minute HFT normalized trading flow, then long the top-tercile stocks and short bottom-tercile stocks, weighted by market capitalization of each stock. The portfolio is held for 60 seconds, with return recorded as $R^{H-L}_{t,t+60}$. The HML portfolio is re-weighted at the beginning of every minute, based on the normalized HFT flow during the last minute. $RV^{MKT}_{t,t+60} - RV^{MKT}_{t-300,t}$ captures the volatility shock, by measuring the increase of return variation from past 300 seconds to future 60 seconds. Column (1) and (2) use HML portfolios generated from all 120 stocks in the sample, while Column (3) to (5) use HML portfolios generated from 40 large/middle/small stocks.

	(1)	(2)	(3)	(4)	(5)
	All Stocks	All Stocks	Large Stocks	Medium Stocks	Small Stocks
Intercept	0.045***	0.045***	0.043***	0.023***	0.205***
	(22.55)	(22.42)	(24.81)	(4.03)	(9.61)
$R^{MKT}_{t,t+60}(\times 10^{-3})$	-16.462***	-16.521***	-29.106***	-16.165***	-37.280***
	(-8.13)	(-8.16)	(-15.29)	(-3.41)	(-2.34)
$RV^{MKT}_{t,t+60} - RV^{MKT}_{t-300,t}(\times 10^{-3})$		-0.254***	-0.357***	-0.193*	-0.151
		(-3.52)	(-4.27)	(-1.95)	(-1.19)
Month Fixed Effect	No	No	No	No	No
N	194700	194700	194700	194700	194700
R-Square	0.001	0.001	0.002	0.001	0.006

Table 5: Regression of HFT portfolio on volatility shock level

Table 6. Robust Test: Regression of HFT portfolio on volatility shock level. All regression setups are identical as in Table 5, except that when calculating HFT high-minus-low return $R_{t,t+60}^{H-L}$, in Table 5 I used $R_{t,t+60}$. I replace P_t with $\tilde{P}_t$, but now I replace P_t with $\tilde{P}_t =$ $\frac{\sum_{HFTtrade \in (t-60,t)} S_t * P_t}{\sum_{HFTtrade \in (t-60,t)} S_t}$, that is, the initial price is now considered as the average execution price during the past 60 seconds, rather than the price at the beginning of portfolio holding period.

	(1)	(2)	(3)	(4)	(5)
	All Stocks	All Stocks	Large Stocks	Medium Stocks	Small Stocks
Intercept	0.352***	0.350***	0.165***	0.104***	0.016
	(23.73)	(23.59)	(69.68)	(7.01)	(0.16)
$R_{t,t+60}^{MKT}(\times10^{-3})$	-21.474***	-11.259***	-22.539***	-15.788***	-17.607***
	(-6.22)	(-4.89)	(-18.50)	(-6.09)	(-3.60)
$RV_{t,t+60}^{MKT} - RV_{t-300,t}^{MKT}(\times10^{-3})$		-0.541***	-0.821***	-0.334***	-0.052
		(-2.37)	(-3.76)	(-2.97)	(-1.21)
Month Fixed Effect	No	No	No	No	No
N	194700	194700	194700	194700	194700
R-Square	0.001	0.003	0.003	0.003	0.002

Table 6: Regression of HFT portfolio on volatility shock level(Robust Test)

Table 7. Robust Test: Regression of daily HFT portfolio on ΔVIX. Regression formula is based on Eq. 7. The HFT high-minus-low portfolio is constructed by ranking HFTs' past-minute normalized trading flow, then long the top-tercile stocks and short bottom-tercile stocks, weighted by market capitalization of each stock. The portfolio is held and re-weighted for every 60 seconds, and the cumulative daily return of this high-minus-low strategy is recorded as R_m^{H-L}. ΔVIX captures the volatility shock, by measuring the change of the CBOE VIX Index from the previous day to the current day. In columns (1) and (2), HFT high-minus-low portfolio is generated from all 120 stocks in the sample, while columns (3) to (5) use the high-minus-low portfolio generated from 40 large/middle/small stocks.

	(1) All Stocks	(2) All Stocks	(3) Large Stocks	(4) Middle Stocks	(5) Small Stocks
Intercept	0.0083***	0.0080	0.0133*	-0.0067	-0.0004
	(16.760)	(1.428)	(1.886)	(-0.370)	(-0.043)
MKT_Coef	0.0318	-0.1088**	-0.1375**	-0.0519	-0.0192
	(1.323)	(-2.083)	(-2.104)	(-1.503)	(-1.144)
Delta_VIX_Coef		-0.0009***	-0.0011***	-0.0005**	-0.0002
		(-2.543)	(-2.431)	(-2.059)	(-1.621)
Month Fixed Effect	No	No	No	No	No
N	504	504	504	504	504
R2	0.003	0.013	0.012	0.012	0.006

Table 7: Regression of HFT daily portfolio on Δ_{VIX} (Robust Test)

Table 8. Prediction of stock future return based on HFTs' speculative-trading style. Regression formula is based on Eq. 9 in the paper. Each observation is from the beginning of each minute during market hours, per stock per trading day. Columns (1) to (3) use observations from all stocks, while columns (4) to (6) only use observations among 40 large/middle/small stocks. For computation purpose, all regression has been done by randomly selecting four million stock-day-minute observations from the entire sample. The last row, "Return increase(%)", calculates the percentage of increase in return by applying all factors from the regression, comparing with the baseline return level by merely longing stocks, after controlling the risk exposure at the same level. See Campbell & Thompson (2008) for more details.

	(1)	(2)	(3)	(4)	(5)	(6)
	All Stocks	All Stocks	All Stocks	Large Stocks	Middle Stocks	Small Stocks
Intercept($\times 10^{-3}$)	0.018***	0.055*	0.018***	0.007***	0.013***	0.034***
	(14.712)	(1.706)	(14.827)	(4.419)	(6.475)	(13.094)
$\tilde{R}^i_{t-60,t}(\times 10^{-3})$	-9.630***	-11.998***	-9.459***	-26.368***	-11.450***	-5.111***
	(-10.454)	(-5.289)	(-10.287)	(-16.660)	(-7.282)	(-3.150)
$HFT\_Flow^i_{t-60,t}(\times 10^{-3})$			0.646***	0.711***	0.704***	0.501***
			(16.328)	(8.372)	(12.515)	(7.455)
Firm Fixed Effect	No	Yes	Yes	Yes	Yes	Yes
Month Fixed Effect	No	No	No	No	No	No
N	4000000	4000000	4000000	4000000	4000000	4000000
R-Square	0.00009	0.00093	0.00369	0.00450	0.00689	0.00319
Return increase(%)	7.487	75.653	299.748	349.207	538.571	262.300

Table 8: Return prediction test from HFT trading flow: speculative trading

Table 9. Prediction of stock future return based on HFTs' liquidity-timing style. Regression formula is based on Eq. 10 in the paper. Each observation is from the beginning of each minute during market hours, per stock per trading day. Columns (1) to (3) use observations from all stocks, while columns (4) to (6) only use observations among 40 large/middle/small stocks. For computation purpose, all regression has been done by randomly selecting four million stock-day-minute observations from the entire sample. The last row, "Return increase(%)", calculates the percentage of increase in return by applying all factors from the regression, comparing with the baseline return level by merely longing stocks, after controlling the risk exposure at the same level. See Campbell & Thompson (2008) for more details.

	(1)	(2)	(3)	(4)	(5)	(6)
	All Stocks	All Stocks	All Stocks	Large Stocks	Middle Stocks	Small Stocks
Intercept($\times 10^{-3}$)	0.018***	0.055*	0.018***	0.007***	0.014***	0.034***
	(14.712)	(1.706)	(14.789)	(4.284)	(6.565)	(13.070)
$\bar{R}^i_{t-60,t}(\times 10^{-3})$	-9.630***	-11.998***	-8.771***	-26.351***	-12.208***	-5.260***
	(-10.454)	(-5.289)	(-9.523)	(-16.349)	(-7.750)	(-3.221)
$Opposite\_flow^i_{t-60,t} * \bar{R}^i_{t-60,t}(\times 10^{-3})$			-153.421***	-169.293***	-244.067***	-127.106***
			(-34.112)	(-14.796)	(-31.571)	(-17.799)
Firm Fixed Effect	No	Yes	Yes	Yes	Yes	Yes
Month Fixed Effect	No	No	No	No	No	No
N	4000000	4000000	4000000	4000000	4000000	4000000
R-Square	0.00009	0.00093	0.00108	0.00283	0.00311	0.00113
Return increase(%)	7.487	75.653	187.211	219.234	242.371	92.224

Table 9: Return prediction test from HFT trading flow: liquidity-timing

Table 10. Robust Test: Prediction of stock future return based on HFTs' speculative-trading style. All regression setups are identical as in Table 8, except that the regression formula is based on Eq. 13 in the paper, with extra terms controlling the past 60~3600s stock excess return.

	(1) All Stocks	(2) All Stocks	(3) All Stocks	(4) Large Stocks	(5) Middle Stocks	(6) Small Stocks
Intercept($\times 10^{-3}$)	0.012***	-0.014	0.012***	0.005***	0.011***	0.022***
	(10.559)	(-0.503)	(10.601)	(2.918)	(5.597)	(8.771)
$\tilde{R}^i_{t-60,t}(\times 10^{-3})$	-19.668***	-20.492***	-19.629***	-25.244***	-25.789***	-4.590***
	(-19.977)	(-9.016)	(-19.978)	(-15.423)	(-15.132)	(-2.602)
$\tilde{R}^i_{t-120,t-60}(\times 10^{-3})$	-0.807	-1.617	1.398	-18.007***	-5.342***	-6.955***
	(-0.814)	(-0.704)	(1.411)	(-10.912)	(-3.110)	(-3.923)
$\tilde{R}^i_{t-300,t-120}(\times 10^{-3})$	0.200	-0.134	0.698	-0.366	-4.928***	-1.757*
	(0.354)	(-0.102)	(1.234)	(-0.371)	(-4.883)	(-1.812)
$\tilde{R}^i_{t-3600,t-300}(\times 10^{-3})$	-0.217	-0.779	-0.223	-0.337	-0.685	-0.156
	(-1.536)	(-1.387)	(-1.579)	(-0.740)	(-1.558)	(-0.840)
$HFT\_Flow^i_{t-60,t}(\times 10^{-3})$			0.610***	0.679***	0.652***	0.483***
			(16.088)	(8.153)	(12.380)	(7.375)
Firm Fixed Effect	No	Yes	Yes	Yes	Yes	Yes
Month Fixed Effect	No	No	No	No	No	No
N	4000000	4000000	4000000	4000000	4000000	4000000
R-Square	0.00042	0.00123	0.00444	0.00484	0.01028	0.00368
Return increase(%)	34.371	99.788	360.998	375.438	806.594	302.539

Table 10: Return prediction test from HFT trading flow: speculative trading (longer past return horizon)

Table 11. Robust Test: Prediction of stock future return based on HFTs' liquidity-timing style. All regression setups are identical as in Table 9, except that the regression formula is based on Eq. 14 in the paper, with extra terms controlling the past 60~3600s stock excess return.

	(1) All Stocks	(2) All Stocks	(3) All Stocks	(4) Large Stocks	(5) Middle Stocks	(6) Small Stocks
Intercept($\times 10^{-3}$)	0.012***	-0.014	0.012***	0.005***	0.011***	0.022***
	(10.559)	(-0.503)	(10.546)	(2.916)	(5.594)	(8.648)
$\tilde{R}^i_{t-60,t}$($\times 10^{-3}$)	-19.668***	-20.492***	-20.569***	-26.912***	-28.470***	-4.443***
	(-19.977)	(-9.016)	(-20.900)	(-16.142)	(-16.626)	(-2.513)
$\tilde{R}^i_{t-120,t-60}$($\times 10^{-3}$)	-0.807	-1.617	-0.070	-18.528***	-7.445***	-6.185***
	(-0.814)	(-0.704)	(-0.070)	(-11.225)	(-4.327)	(-3.486)
$\tilde{R}^i_{t-300,t-120}$($\times 10^{-3}$)	0.200	-0.134	0.411	-0.591	-5.171***	-1.586
	(0.354)	(-0.102)	(0.726)	(-0.598)	(-5.112)	(-1.634)
$\tilde{R}^i_{t-3600,t-300}$($\times 10^{-3}$)	-0.217	-0.779	-0.218	-0.316	-0.675	-0.154
	(-1.536)	(-1.387)	(-1.543)	(-0.693)	(-1.533)	(-0.826)
$Opposite\_Flow^i_{t-60,t} * \tilde{R}^i_{t-60,t}$($\times 10^{-3}$)			-166.841***	-277.672***	-217.765***	-139.161***
			(-35.978)	(-23.387)	(-29.540)	(-18.119)
Firm Fixed Effect	No	Yes	Yes	Yes	Yes	Yes
Month Fixed Effect	No	No	No	No	No	No
N	4000000	4000000	4000000	4000000	4000000	4000000
R-Square	0.00042	0.00123	0.00168	0.00396	0.00565	0.00144
Return increase(%)	34.371	99.788	236.469	306.589	441.116	118.445

Table 11: Return prediction test from HFT trading flow: liquidity-timing (longer past return horizon)

Table 12. Summary of key regression coefficients from stock events. All selected news events are categorized into different topics based on variable "Group" assigned to each event from RavenPack. For regression results, The speculative-trading coefficient, ϕ, is based from Eq. 16; The liquidity-timing coefficient, γ, is based from Eq. 17; The market-making coefficient, β, is based from Eq. 15. N represents number of news observations under each news topic group. For clarity purpose, all news groups are sorted by the level of ϕ coefficients.

Topics	$\phi(\times10^{-3})$	Tstat	$\gamma(\times10^{-3})$	Tstat	β	Tstat	N
(All topics)	1.225***	(2.733)	-19.544***	(-6.784)	-3.208***	(-2.710)	25419
Acquisitions-mergers	2.665***	(5.108)	-318.485***	(-5.665)	4.647	(1.182)	1412
Investor-relations	1.639***	(2.616)	-5.855	(-0.058)	6.572	(0.729)	455
Analyst-ratings	1.631***	(3.528)	-81.061**	(-2.093)	3.105	(0.722)	1244
Revenues	1.529***	(3.007)	-46.336	(-1.598)	18.360	(1.600)	2724
Credit-ratings	1.440***	(2.998)	-401.153***	(-2.428)	-3.669	(-1.004)	1045
Earnings	1.386***	(3.578)	-48.488**	(-2.160)	-1.520	(-0.363)	3755
Insider-trading	0.985***	(6.994)	-107.158***	(-5.444)	-3.222	(-1.134)	5112
Labor-issues	0.970***	(3.044)	7.228	(0.153)	9.581***	(3.310)	1577
Products-services	0.647***	(3.408)	1.519	(0.089)	-5.227	(-1.544)	3762
Dividends	0.563	(0.585)	24.728	(0.383)	3.407	(0.737)	290
Marketing	0.542	(1.148)	24.009	(0.283)	-7.281	(-0.723)	226
Legal	0.425	(1.097)	-42.955	(-1.094)	-13.491***	(-2.572)	676
Partnerships	-0.240	(-0.804)	29.090	(1.212)	-13.283***	(-2.675)	640
Technical-analysis	-0.377	(-1.235)	47.226	(1.119)	-10.047**	(-2.239)	646
Stock-prices	-0.803*	(-1.876)	16.212	(0.578)	-11.683*	(-1.658)	710
Equity-actions	-0.994	(-0.880)	91.322	(1.554)	-12.289***	(-3.461)	640

Table 12: Event study: Regression coefficient summary

Table 13. **Two-fold validation of speculative-trading coefficients in news events study.** All selected news events are categorized into different topics based on the variable "Group" assigned to each event from RavenPack. The speculative trading coefficient, ϕ, is based from Eq. 16; N represents number of news observations under each news topic group. Column "All Data" represents regression results from all events under each topic; column "Year 2008" (or "Year 2009") represents regression results from all events within the Year 2008 (or Year 2009) under each topic. For clarity purpose, all news are sorted by the level of ϕ coefficients in Table 12.

Topics	All Data			Year 2008			Year 2009		
	$\phi(\times10^{-3})$	Tstat	N	$\phi(\times10^{-3})$	Tstat	N	$\phi(\times10^{-3})$	Tstat	N
Acquisitions-mergers	2.665***	(5.108)	1412	2.482***	(4.147)	797	2.796***	(4.511)	615
Investor-relations	1.639***	(2.616)	455	2.231***	(3.141)	214	1.413**	(2.142)	241
Analyst-ratings	1.631***	(3.528)	1244	0.915***	(3.008)	592	1.977***	(6.388)	652
Revenues	1.529***	(3.007)	2724	1.525***	(2.760)	1430	1.529***	(2.814)	1294
Credit-ratings	1.440***	(2.998)	1045	1.117**	(2.116)	354	1.506***	(3.202)	691
Earnings	1.386***	(3.578)	3755	1.663***	(3.752)	1739	0.937**	(2.227)	2016
Insider-trading	0.985***	(6.994)	5112	1.145***	(7.015)	2720	0.595***	(3.601)	2392
Labor-issues	0.970***	(3.044)	1577	0.943***	(2.576)	823	1.267***	(3.691)	754
Products-services	0.647***	(3.408)	3762	0.638***	(3.136)	1627	0.659***	(2.939)	2135
Dividends	0.563	(0.585)	290	0.228	(0.225)	126	0.656	(0.553)	164
Marketing	0.542	(1.148)	226	0.701	(1.313)	126	0.196	(0.384)	100
Legal	0.425	(1.097)	676	0.273	(0.624)	250	0.461	(0.998)	426
Partnerships	-0.240	(-0.804)	640	-0.147	(-0.433)	290	-0.306	(-1.031)	350
Technical-analysis	-0.377	(-1.235)	646	-0.009	(-0.026)	408	-0.520	(-1.550)	238
Stock-prices	-0.803*	(-1.876)	710	-2.052***	(-4.173)	360	-0.620	(-1.176)	350
Equity-actions	-0.994	(-0.880)	640	-0.933	(-0.790)	337	-2.837**	(-1.980)	303

Table 13: Event study: Twofold validation on speculative-trading coefficients

Table 14. Two-fold validation of market-making coefficients in news events study. All selected news events are categorized into different topics based on the variable "Group" assigned to each event from RavenPack. The liquidity-timing coefficient, γ, is based from Eq. 17. N represents the number of news observations under each news topic group. Column "All Data" represents regression results from all events under each topic; column "Year 2008" (or "Year 2009") represents regression results from all events within the Year 2008 (or Year 2009) under each topic. For clarity purpose, all news are sorted by the level of ϕ coefficients in Table 12.

Topics	All Data			Year 2008			Year 2009		
	$\gamma(\times10^{-3})$	Tstat	N	$\gamma(\times10^{-3})$	Tstat	N	$\gamma(\times10^{-3})$	Tstat	N
Acquisitions-mergers	-318.485***	(-5.665)	1412	-340.577***	(-5.878)	797	-292.211***	(-3.719)	615
Investor-relations	-5.855	(-0.058)	455	-9.189	(-0.084)	214	11.034	(0.091)	241
Analyst-ratings	-81.061**	(-2.093)	1244	-99.844***	(-2.440)	592	-76.761*	(-1.838)	652
Revenues	-46.336	(-1.598)	2724	-33.870	(-1.076)	1430	-52.319*	(-1.655)	1294
Credit-ratings	-401.153***	(-2.428)	1045	-381.500**	(-2.072)	354	-414.669***	(-2.577)	691
Earnings	-48.488**	(-2.160)	3755	-40.041	(-1.650)	1739	-54.607**	(-2.271)	2016
Insider-trading	-107.158***	(-5.444)	5112	-101.004***	(-4.574)	2720	-115.899***	(-4.841)	2392
Labor-issues	7.228	(0.153)	1577	42.015	(0.734)	823	-57.477	(-1.085)	754
Products-services	1.519	(0.089)	3762	19.039	(1.039)	1627	-29.967	(-1.559)	2135
Dividends	24.728	(0.383)	290	84.591	(1.176)	126	-26.091	(-0.371)	164
Marketing	24.009	(0.283)	226	30.124	(0.313)	126	19.443	(0.217)	100
Legal	-42.955	(-1.094)	676	-23.303	(-0.570)	250	-46.722	(-1.022)	426
Partnerships	29.090	(1.212)	640	43.068	(1.544)	290	-26.768	(-1.010)	350
Technical-analysis	47.226	(1.119)	646	40.233	(0.824)	408	60.910	(1.322)	238
Stock-prices	16.212	(0.578)	710	8.643	(0.294)	360	21.040	(0.595)	350
Equity-actions	91.322	(1.554)	640	27.682	(0.423)	337	174.428**	(2.111)	303

Table 14: Event study: Twofold validation on market-making coefficients

Table 15. **Stock return variation around event time under each topic.** All selected news events are categorized into different topics based on variable "Group" assigned to each event from RavenPack. $RV_{a,b}$ measures the standard deviation of 10s return from time $t = a$ to time $t = b$. For comparison purpose, $Ratio\_Xs$ is defined as $RV_{0,x}/RV_{-X,0}$. A ratio larger than one implies the stock volatility increases after events occur. N represents number of news observations under each news topic group. For clarity purpose, all news topics are sorted in the same order as in Table 12.

Topics	$RV_{-300,0}$	$RV_{-120,0}$	$RV_{-60,0}$	$RV_{0,60}$	$RV_{0,120}$	$RV_{0,300}$	Ratio_60s	Ratio_120s	Ratio_300s	N
(All topics)	30.92	34.57	39.04	35.45	30.38	25.54	0.91	0.88	0.83	25419
(No equity-actions)	56.59	57.28	58.69	70.10	62.96	53.67	1.19	1.10	0.95	24779
Acquisitions-mergers	28.10	29.71	29.66	44.30	37.58	32.70	1.49	1.26	1.16	1412
Investor-relations	21.26	26.24	27.00	32.81	27.82	23.26	1.21	1.06	1.09	455
Analyst-ratings	98.24	92.82	78.14	83.31	75.59	70.88	1.07	0.81	0.72	1244
Revenues	124.54	124.04	136.45	152.01	125.89	97.40	1.11	1.01	0.78	2724
Credit-ratings	42.43	41.45	38.78	50.87	55.53	46.72	1.31	1.34	1.10	1045
Earnings	87.43	84.98	89.15	134.90	115.22	93.48	1.51	1.36	1.07	3755
Insider-trading	20.73	21.74	21.78	24.66	23.42	22.50	1.13	1.08	1.09	5112
Labor-issues	46.43	42.50	38.25	37.55	39.76	37.23	0.98	0.94	0.80	1577
Products-services	38.74	38.54	38.03	42.77	41.09	38.39	1.12	1.07	0.99	3762
Dividends	115.88	161.67	153.92	148.44	124.68	114.47	0.96	0.77	0.99	290
Marketing	20.65	23.21	22.20	20.14	21.01	23.34	0.91	0.91	1.13	226
Legal	32.96	49.63	78.95	64.13	53.67	34.20	0.81	1.08	1.04	676
Partnerships	36.94	40.20	38.79	39.53	42.74	46.42	1.02	1.06	1.26	640
Technical-analysis	21.64	20.93	22.53	21.90	20.57	20.63	0.97	0.98	0.95	646
Stock-prices	94.49	102.20	97.30	98.72	112.87	98.39	1.01	1.10	1.04	710
Equity-actions	645.41	949.38	1299.11	541.99	355.03	270.49	0.42	0.37	0.42	640

Table 15: Event study: Return variation around events

Table 16. **Summary statistics: Fraction of trade, volume and cumulative price change across trade sizes and identity of traders.** Results are from all trading records across 120 stocks in NASDAQ HFT Dataset, from the Year 2008 to 2009. For columns, "Trade", "Volume" and "CumPChange" calculate the fraction of the number of trading records, trading shares, and cumulative price change within each subgroup. "Before", "At", "After" correspond to trading statistics before/at/after market hours, and Column "AllTime" corresponds to trading statistics throughout all periods. For rows, statistics are shown within each subgroup differing by trading size (e.g., "≤ 100" means all trades with sizes no larger than 100 shares). Rows "Small", "Middle", "Large" calculate statistics among trades with size ≤ 500, $>500\& \leq10000$, and >10000. Rows "HH", "HN", "NH", "NN" calculates statistics among trades differing by types of liquidity-takers and liquidity-makers.

	Trades				Volume				CumPChange			
	Before(%)	At(%)	After(%)	AllTime(%)	Before(%)	At(%)	After(%)	AllTime(%)	Before(%)	At(%)	After(%)	AllTime(%)
≤100	17.78	12.60	18.21	12.65	1.49	1.18	1.48	1.18	1.88	25.87	0.31	28.06
$>100\&\leq200$	34.21	43.98	33.83	43.89	7.76	12.04	7.68	11.99	2.47	42.15	1.64	46.26
$>200\&\leq300$	13.53	15.77	13.84	15.75	6.04	8.55	6.18	8.52	0.72	6.62	0.75	8.09
$>300\&\leq400$	6.51	7.15	7.00	7.15	4.33	5.80	4.65	5.79	0.28	4.78	0.61	5.67
$>400\&\leq500$	4.02	4.77	4.21	4.77	3.55	5.14	3.72	5.13	0.17	1.63	0.32	2.13
$>500\&\leq600$	6.44	3.30	6.65	3.32	6.97	4.43	7.20	4.45	0.32	-0.49	0.16	-0.02
$>600\&\leq1000$	5.48	5.56	5.35	5.56	8.76	10.68	8.52	10.66	0.24	5.49	0.45	6.17
$>1000\&\leq2000$	7.62	4.06	6.77	4.09	19.30	13.92	17.33	13.97	0.31	0.98	0.55	1.84
$>2000\&\leq5000$	3.25	1.96	3.01	1.97	19.67	15.36	18.38	15.40	0.17	0.48	0.38	1.04
$>5000\&\leq10000$	0.86	0.55	0.77	0.56	11.32	9.83	10.43	9.84	0.05	0.29	0.17	0.51
>10000	0.30	0.29	0.36	0.29	10.79	13.07	14.42	13.07	0.01	0.24	0.01	0.26
HH	4.12	18.15	7.38	18.05	2.13	16.33	3.86	16.19	0.19	-1.10	0.37	-0.54
HN	15.13	29.93	19.25	29.82	10.16	22.09	14.10	21.99	0.33	8.94	1.35	10.62
NH	14.96	22.82	15.79	22.76	12.22	33.42	14.85	33.21	0.50	23.12	-0.68	22.94
NN	65.79	29.09	57.58	29.37	75.49	28.15	67.19	28.61	5.59	57.08	4.31	66.97
Small	76.04	84.28	77.09	84.21	23.18	32.71	23.71	32.61	5.52	81.05	3.63	90.20
Middle	23.65	15.43	22.56	15.50	66.03	54.22	61.88	54.33	1.09	6.75	1.70	9.54
Large	0.30	0.29	0.36	0.29	10.79	13.07	14.42	13.07	0.01	0.24	0.01	0.26
Total	100.00	100.00	100.00	100.00	100.00	100.00	100.00	100.00	6.61	88.04	5.35	100.00

Table 16: All data: Fraction of cumulative price change, volume and trades based on trade sizes and identity of traders

Table 17. Fraction of cumulative price change, volume and trades based on liquidity-takers under each topic. All selected news events are categorized into different topics based on the variable "Group" assigned to each event from RavenPack. All metrics are calculated based on whether the liquidity-taker is HFTs ("HX") or non-HFTs ("NX"). "CumPChange(%)" calculates the fraction of 0~300s stock price change attribution, "Volume(%)" calculates the fraction of 0~300s trading shares, "Trades(%)" calculates the fraction of 0~300s trades. For clarity purpose, all news topics are sorted in the same order as in Table 12.

Topics	HX_CumPChange(%)	NX_CumPChange(%)	HX_Volume(%)	NX_Volume(%)	HX_Trades(%)	NX_Trades(%)
Acquisitions-mergers	38.09	61.91	36.27	62.91	49.30	49.30
Investor-relations	36.24	63.76	32.70	67.30	54.72	54.72
Analyst-ratings	39.84	60.16	35.12	63.42	49.04	49.04
Revenues	38.09	61.91	33.91	65.69	46.47	46.47
Credit-ratings	35.25	64.75	39.33	60.53	51.61	51.61
Earnings	31.33	68.67	33.92	65.75	45.72	45.72
Insider-trading	35.00	65.00	34.55	64.97	49.43	49.43
Labor-issues	34.72	65.28	35.39	63.74	50.77	50.77
Products-services	29.74	70.26	40.11	59.33	48.50	48.50
Dividends	26.81	73.19	38.79	61.21	53.50	53.50
Marketing	31.09	68.91	34.60	63.37	54.18	54.18
Legal	29.56	70.44	36.54	62.69	48.09	48.09
Partnerships	27.62	72.38	35.76	62.16	51.72	51.72
Technical-analysis	29.86	70.14	35.33	64.45	46.38	46.38
Stock-prices	26.97	73.03	36.93	62.62	48.60	48.60
Equity-actions	23.26	76.74	31.58	67.76	48.35	48.35

Table 17: Event study: Fraction of cumulative price change, volume and trades based on liquidity-takers

70

Table 18. Test of price persistence during news events. All selected news events are categorized into different topics based on the variable "Group" assigned to each event from RavenPack. Table lists the auto-correlation of stock return around news events (where the event time is recorded as 0s), under each different topic subgroup. For columns, "$\rho_{a,b}$" are calculated as the correlation of stock return between 0~30s stock return versus returns within seconds a to b around event time. For example, column "$\rho_{-30,0}$" represents correlation of return between 0~30s and -30~0s. For clarity purpose, all news topics are sorted in the same order as in Table 12.

Topics	$\rho_{-30,0}$	$\rho_{30,300}$	$\rho_{300,900}$
Acquisitions-mergers	0.132	0.611	0.268
Investor-relations	0.218	0.675	0.360
Analyst-ratings	0.236	0.758	0.250
Revenues	0.076	0.711	0.363
Credit-ratings	0.044	0.662	0.142
Earnings	0.043	0.663	0.325
Insider-trading	0.048	0.489	0.276
Labor-issues	0.164	0.626	0.125
Products-services	0.172	0.539	0.061
Dividends	0.098	0.489	0.177
Marketing	0.280	0.497	0.102
Legal	0.067	0.543	-0.041
Partnerships	0.177	0.533	-0.060
Technical-analysis	0.160	0.269	0.410
Stock-prices	-0.239	0.433	0.127
Equity-actions	0.241	0.568	0.106

Table 18: Event study: Test of price persistence around news event time

Figure 1. Fraction of shares and trades from HFTs as liquidity-taker throughout the sample period. Figure (a) plots the fraction of shares where HFTs demand liquidity for each month, and figure (b) plots the fraction of trades. Each plot is done separately within 40 large stocks, 40 middle stocks, 40 and small stocks defined by NASDAQ HFT Dataset. Plots show that HFTs' shares (or trades) account for around 45% in large stocks, 30% in middle stocks, and 15% in small stocks. Though not shown in the figure, the fraction of trades and shares where HFTs demand liquidity also shows a similar pattern.

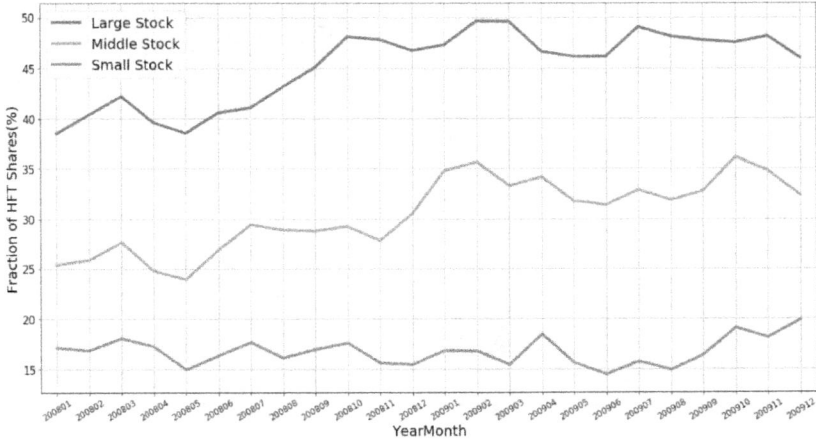

Figure (a): Fraction of trades

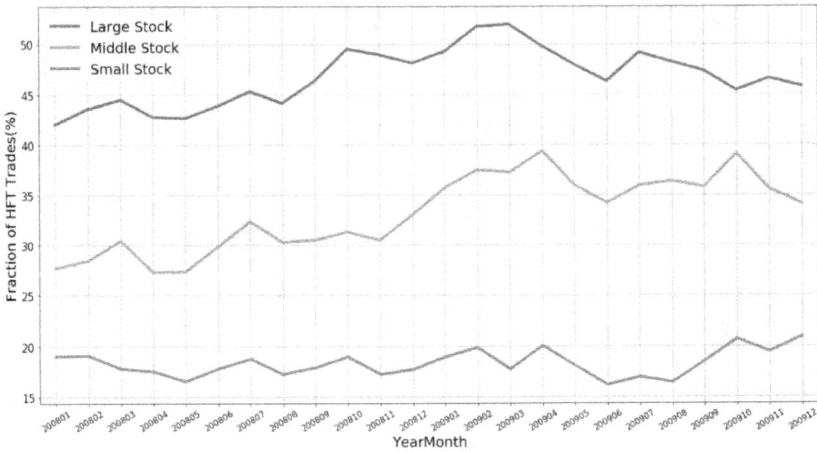

Figure (b): Fraction of trades

Figure 1: Fraction of shares and trades from HFTs as liquidity-takers

Figure 2. Trading return under various liquidation horizons. All trades are categorized into four different subgroups: HH, HN, NH, NN, with the first (second) letter indicating the identity of liquidity-taker (liquidity-maker). For example, HN means liquidity taker is an HFT and liquidity maker is a non-HFT. The X-axis represents the log-value of liquidation time horizons after trades happen (from 0s to 500s), and Y-axis represents the volume-weighted, fee-adjusted average percentage return for the liquidity-taker of trades. Return is calculated in round-trade fashion, that is, return for a buy(sell)-trade if the position is reverted with the NBBO price level at the end of the liquidation time horizon. Dash line represents 95% confidence interval of average return estimation.

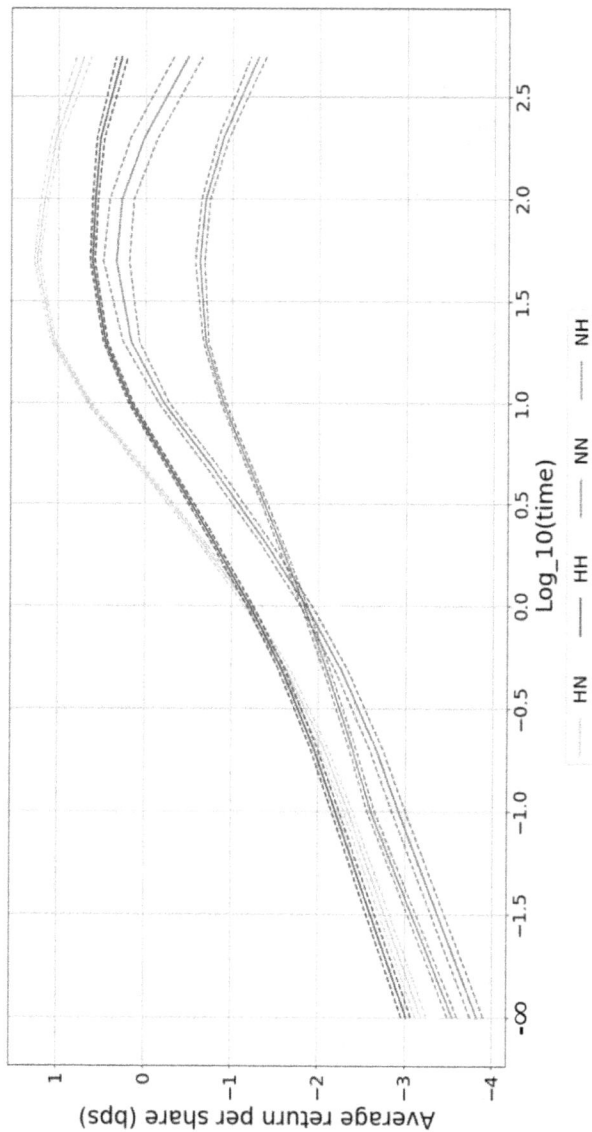

Figure 2: Trading return under various liquidation horizons

Figure 3. Evolution of cumulative price change from different liquidity-takers. Figure shows the evolution of cumulative price change after events, from trades where liquidity-takers are HFTs (red lines) or non-HFTs (blue lines). The sign of Y-value is positive if cumulative price change aligns with the direction of 300-second stock price changes after the corresponding event. Solid lines represent results from all events under the "Informative News" subgroup ("Acquisition-mergers", "Investor-relations", "Analyst-ratings", "Revenues", "Credit-ratings", "Earnings", "Insider-trading", "Labor-issues"), and dashed lines represent results from all events under the "Noisy News" subgroup ("Products-services", "Dividends", "Marketing", "Legal", "Partnership", "Technical-analysis", "Stock-prices", "Equity-actions").

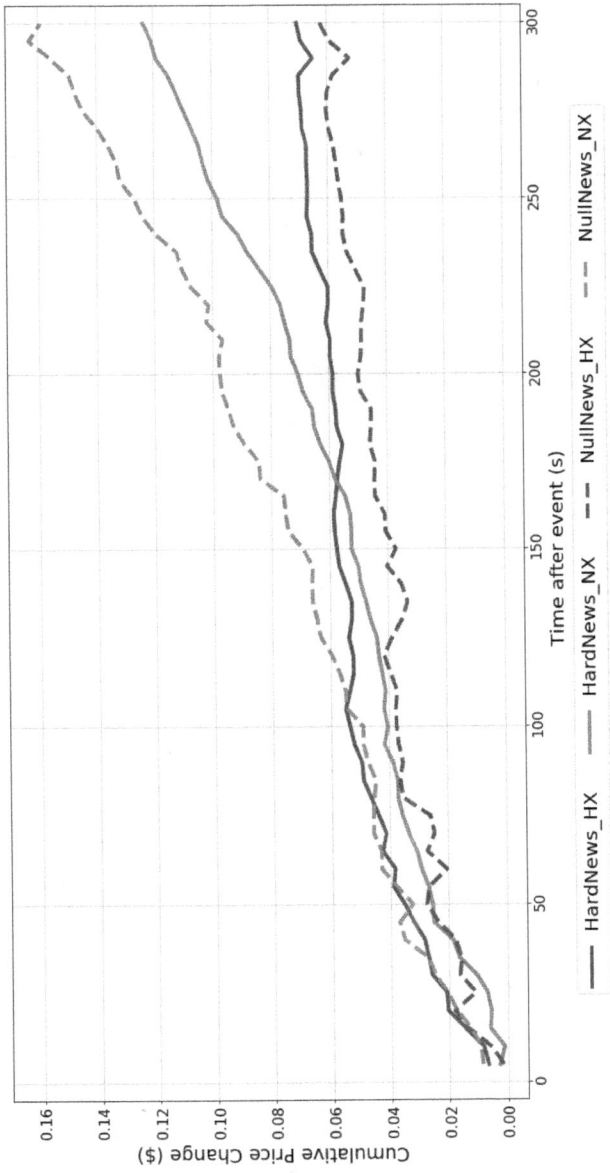

Figure 3: Evolution of cumulative price change from different liquidity-takers

Figure 4. Evolution of average **HFT/non-HFT signed inventory level around event time**. Calculation of HFTs' inventory is based on Eq. 2, by aggregating HFTs' net positions during the period around news events, then being normalized by the average minute-wise volume during the past five calendar days before events. The sign of inventory level is flipped if the 300-second cumulative price change after an event is negative. Due to the structure of the dataset, non-HFTs' inventory is the opposite level to HFTs' inventory. Dashed lines represents 95% confidence interval of the inventory level. For comparison purpose, the HFT cumulative inventory is set to be zero at $t = 0$.

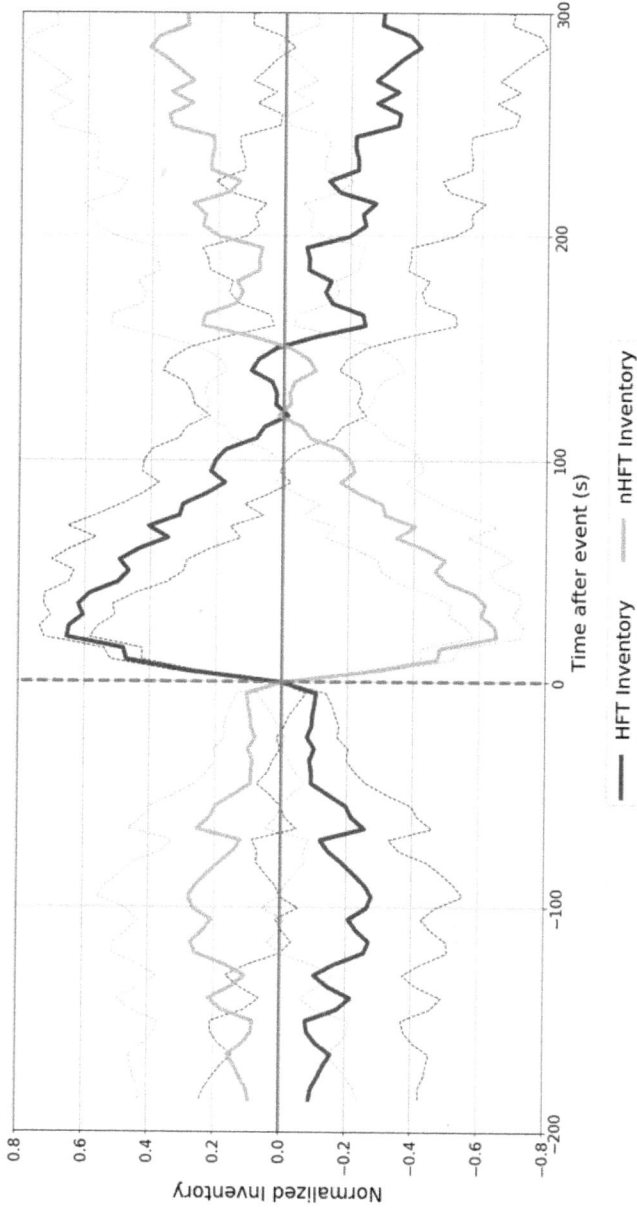

Figure 4: Evolution of average HFT/non-HFT inventory around event time

Figure 5. Evolution of the distribution of trading frequency after events. Results are generated from news events within the "Informative News" group. Each stacked bar shows the percentage distribution of the number of trades, for each event under each 10-second time window. For example, the bar labeled with "0_10s" represents the distribution of the number of trades within 0~10s after event timestamp. Different colors show the percentage of events within different subgroups. Figure (a) shows the distribution from trades where the liquidity-takers are HFTs (HX), and Figure (b) shows the distribution from trades where the liquidity-takers are non-HFTs (NX).

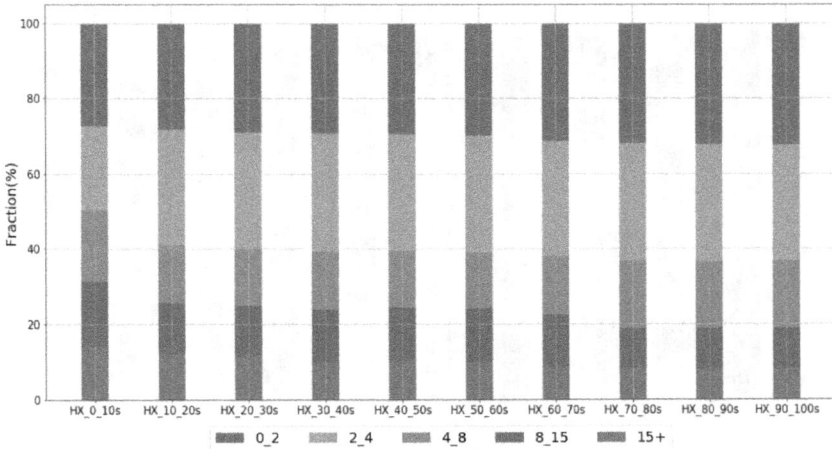

Figure (a): HX Trades

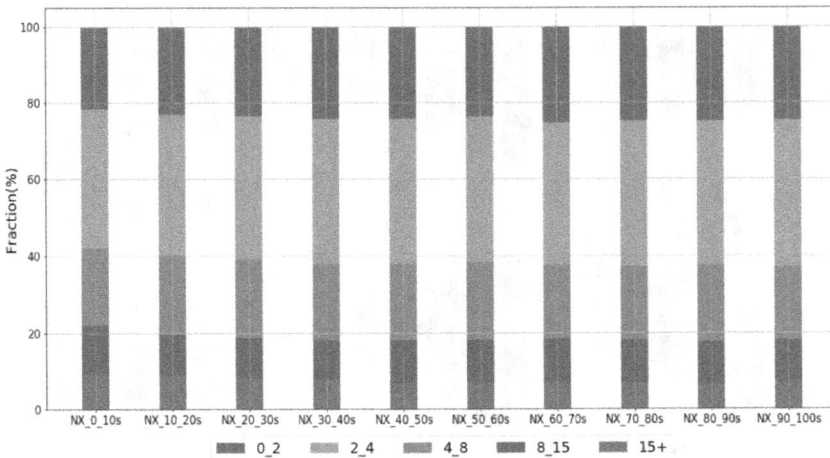

Figure (b): NX Trades

Figure 5: Evolution of distribution of number of trades after events

Figure 6. Evolution of the distribution of average trading size after events. Results are generated from news events within the "Informative News" group. Each stacked bar shows the percentage distribution of average trading size, for each event under each 10-second time window. For example, the bar labeled with "0_10s" represents the distribution of average trading size within 0~10s after event timestamp. Different colors show the percentage of events within different subgroups. Figure (a) shows the distribution from trades where the liquidity-takers are HFTs (HX), and Figure (b) shows the distribution from trades where the liquidity-takers are non-HFTs (NX).

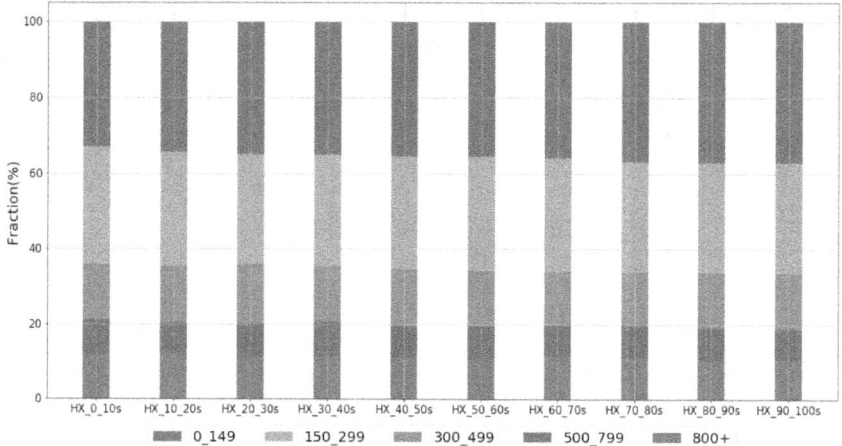

Figure (a): HX Trades

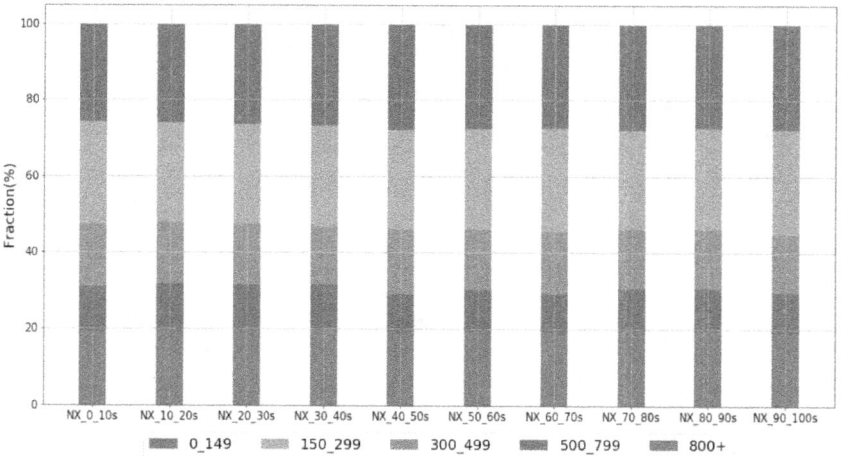

Figure (b): NX Trades

Figure 6: Evolution of distribution of average trading size after events

Figure 7. Evolution of cumulative price changes from sub-events. Plots are under the same logic as was shown in Figure 3, but only among the "Informative News" events under specific criteria. Figure (a) only shows results from events targeting financial stocks (11,031 events); Figure (b) further shows results from events targeting financial stocks, and also happened between 09/18/2008 to 10/12/2008, when SEC temporarily imposes short sales restrictions (532 events).

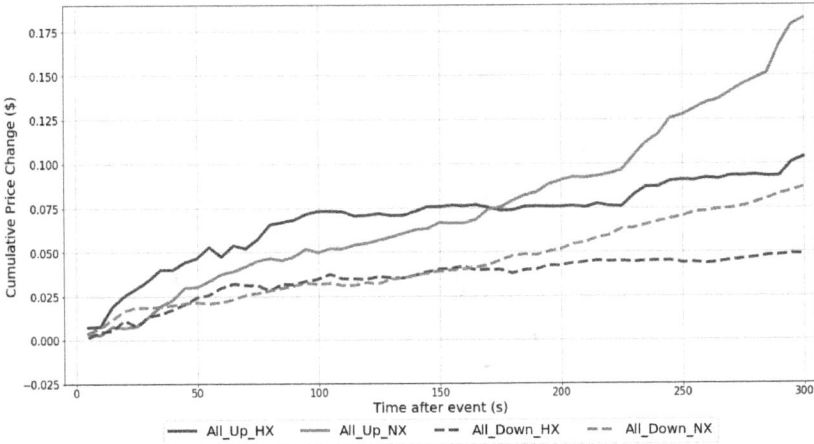

Figure (a): Cumulative price change: Financial stocks

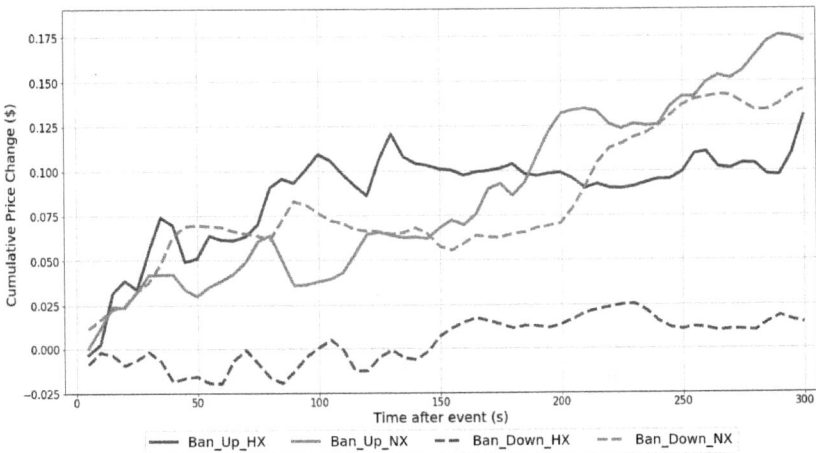

Figure (b): Cumulative price change: Financial stocks within short sales restriction period

Figure 7: Evolution of cumulative price change from sub-events

Figure 8. Evolution of price impact per 100 trading shares. All results are calculated from events in the "Informative News" subgroup, from 0~300s after events occur. Figure (a) shows the results from events with 300s cumulative price change larger than the medium level, and Figure (b) shows the results from events with 300s cumulative price change smaller than the medium level. The red line (blue line) represents results from trades where the identity of liquidity-taker is HFTs (non-HFTs).

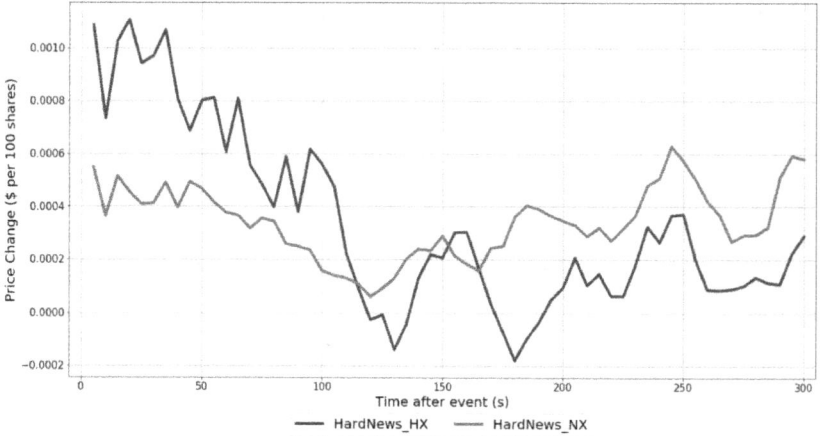

Figure (a): Events with 300s cumulative price change larger than the medium level

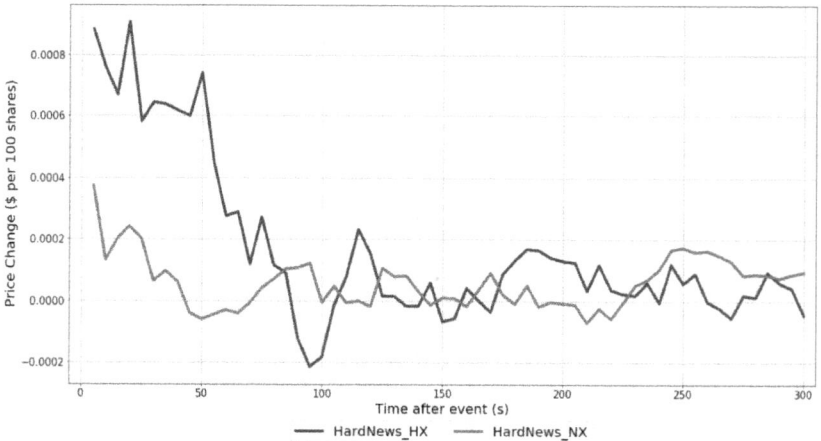

Figure (b): Events with 300s cumulative price change smaller than the medium level

Figure 8: Event study: Price impact per 100 trading shares

Figure 9. Evolution of price impact per trade. All results are calculated from events in the "Informative News" subgroup, from 0~300s after events occur. Figure (a) shows the results from events with 300s cumulative price change larger than the medium level, and Figure (b) shows the results from events with 300s cumulative price change smaller than the medium level. The red line (blue line) represents results from trades where the identity of liquidity-taker is HFTs (non-HFTs).

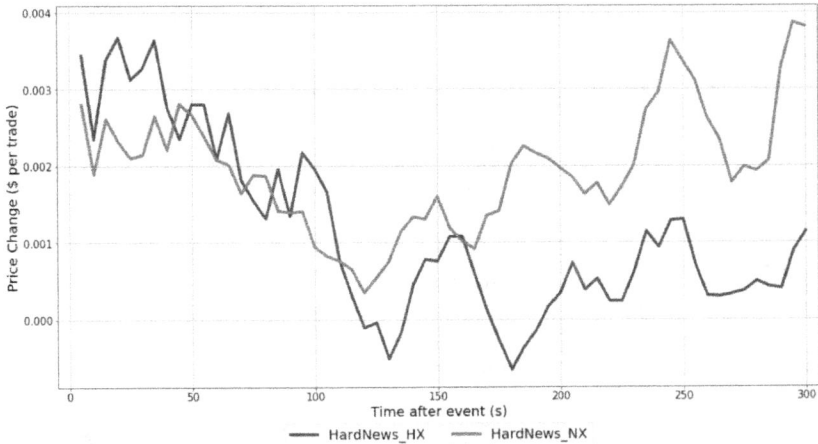

Figure (a): Events with 300s cumulative price change larger than the medium level

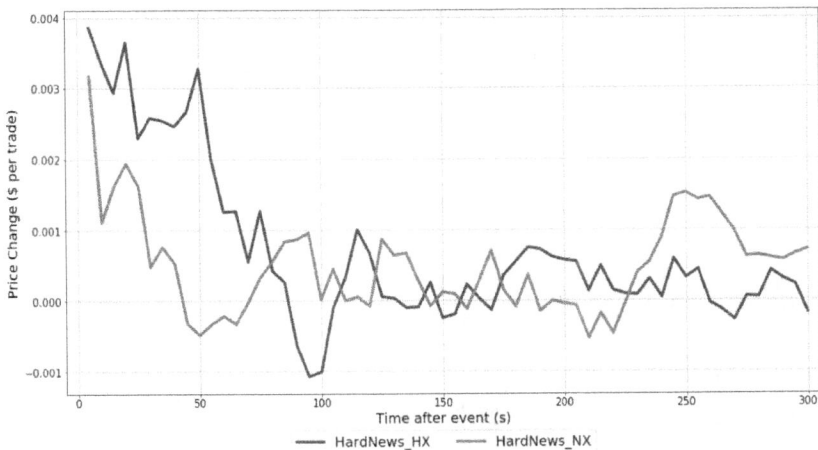

Figure (b): Events with 300s cumulative price change smaller than the medium level

Figure 9: Event study: Price impact per trade

Figure 10. Evolution of average volume and trades after events. Blue lines (Red lines) represent results where liquidity-takers are HFTs (non-HFTs). Solid lines (Dash lines) represent results from events under the "Informative News" ("Noisy News") subgroup.

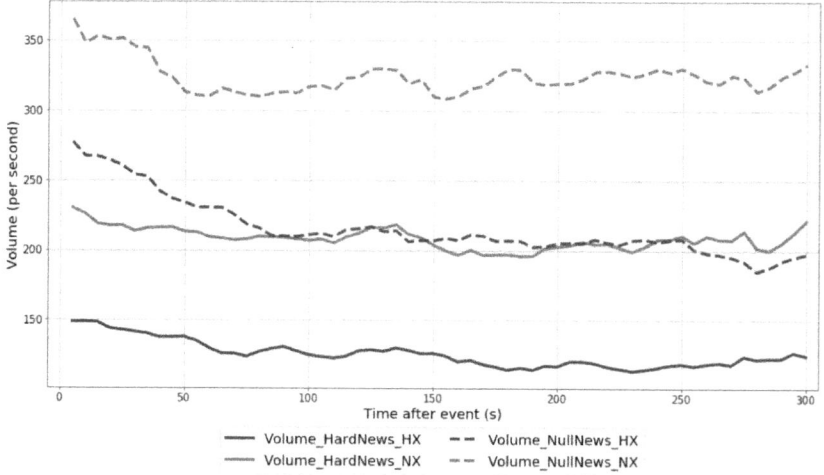

Figure (a): Average volume per second

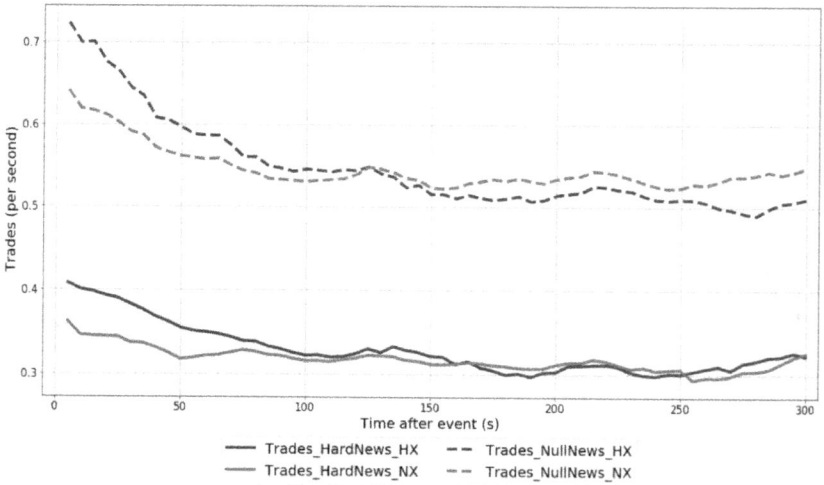

Figure (b): Average trades per second

Figure 10: Event study: Evolution of average volume and trades after events

www.ingramcontent.com/pod-product-compliance
Lightning Source LLC
Chambersburg PA
CBHW071439210326
41597CB00020B/3865